— GOD BLESS YOU —

Endorsements

2 TIMOTHY 1:7

I0631268

"Fear…we all wrestle with it to some degree in our lives. Fear invites you to live a small and somewhat timid lifestyle. In his book, Dr. Ken Nichols, will help you untie the fear knots in your heart. You will learn how to help others who struggle with the manipulation and intimidation of fear."

DR. TIM CLINTON
President
American Association of Christian Counselors

"Dr. Ken Nichols is a personal friend and professional colleague. His style, candor and wisdom ministers to hurting hearts and lives are changed. I wholeheartedly and enthusiastically recommend this life-impacting book. As a Christian psychologist, I am familiar with how fear can literally cause emotional paralysis and spiritual discouragement. This book provides hope and help that is wrapped around the "Fear Not" promises of God's Word."

DR. KEVIN LEMAN
Best-Selling Author and Conference Speaker

"I have known Dr. Ken Nichols for nearly twenty five years. It is a privilege of mine to recommend this tremendous book on fear. In my own personal journey I have been confronted with the power and pressure of unwanted fears. His wise counsel has encouraged me personally. Ken's writing style is reflective of his personal enthusiasm and spiritual zeal. The end-of-chapter application is especially helpful. This book could change your life forever!"

KEN DAVIS
Author, Communicator

"Dr. Ken Nichols applies many biblical principles to the most common causes of debilitating fear. I only wish such a book was available when I was active in counseling, for I would have confidently shared it freely with those whose lives were limited by fear."

TIM LAHAYE
President, Family Life Seminars, Best Selling Author

Untie the
FEAR KNOTS
...of Your Heart

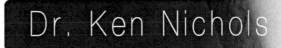

Dr. Ken Nichols

FOREWORD BY DAVID JEREMIAH

LIBERTY
UNIVERSITY
BOOKS

Untie the Fear Knots of Your Heart...
by Dr. Ken Nichols
© Copyright 2010. All rights reserved.

ISBN-13: 978-1-935986-00-3

Cover & Interior Design:

Megan Johnson
Johnson2Design
Johnson2Design.com

LIBERTY
UNIVERSITY
BOOKS
A Division of Liberty University Press
Lynchburg, VA

Dedication

My wife Marlene has been such a faithful source of encouragement and strength. We have been partners in ministry and marriage for over 44 years. Her patience with the time investment this project required and her timely reminders that God will impact lives through it, encouraged me to write and rewrite. I am such a blessed man and am so thankful for my children and grandchildren. We can see the work of the Heavenly Father in each of their lives. A special expression of gratitude and love for my parents who provided a solid foundation, who taught by example, whose love for God and family was contagious and most importantly, whose prayer support is at the core of God's blessing on our lives and ministry.

Acknowledgments

The decision to write this book was the result of much encouragement from David Jeremiah. His commitment to excellence, passion for ministry and genuine enthusiasm for writing is contagious. I am grateful for the faithful friends of ALIVE Ministries who provided the financial support for this project. I owe a special thanks and genuine appreciation to Carol Lacy, who co-labored with me on the first printing of this book many years ago, to Dr. Ron Barnes who provided wise counsel and excellent direction for the biblical content and to my daughter Kara for her valued input and editorial influence on the original fear book project.

This third edition has experienced a major editorial "makeover". I am deeply grateful to Randy Petersen, professional writer/editor, who added insight, a contemporary style and excellent editorial direction. His handiwork is evident in the content from cover to cover.

TABLE OF CONTENTS

Foreword
DAVID JEREMIAH

To live is to face fear. Sometimes there is valid reason for it. On other occasions we are just caught by surprise. Sometimes our fears are imagined and not real. But the effect upon our system is usually the same whether there is any basis for our fear or not.

In my thirty-five years as a Pastor-teacher, I have encountered many varieties of fear. I have been with families as some tragic news is communicated and watched fear paralyze. I have been in the hospital room when the doctor has told his patient that the illness is serious and perhaps life threatening. I have counseled parents whose children have run away! I have tried to help spouses who have just been told that their partner has unexpectedly filed for divorce! I have been present when a doctor has told two young parents that something is wrong with their newborn.

I have stood in front of large crowds to speak and have been personally filled with fear. I have been stabbed to the heart with fear as I have seen my sons take vicious hits on the football field and then just lie there for what seemed like hours. I stayed all night with my daughter Jennifer in the hospital room after she had been injured in a soccer game, suffering a severe concussion. I have watched as my own children entered a new classroom situation for the first time! I have prayed as I dropped my high school graduates off at a faraway college for further education and sensed their twinge of fear that says, "What if I don't fit in here? What if I'm not accepted?"

I have also personally known the kind of fear that grips one's whole system when he is told that he has a serious disease. Fear is not a stranger to me and probably not to you either. You picked up this book because it resonated with something you have experienced personally or shared deeply with another. If we're honest we're all a lot like the little boy who had a part in the school play that read, "It is I, be not afraid." He came out on stage and said, "It's me and I'm scared."

What about Christians and fear? Should we ever fear? Can fear ever be conquered? What do we say to those we know who are being crippled by this emotion? Can fear really be harnessed into something productive and good? The answers to many of these questions are in your hands in this book by my friend, Dr. Ken Nichols. With a conviction born out of many hours of study and personal counseling, he challenges us to turn our fear into faith! He dares us to take something threatening and turn it into something thrilling!

For over twenty-five years I have worked alongside Dr. Nichols and have observed his deep love for the Word of God and for the people of God. Often we have shared together the joy of devoting our lives to the eternal Word of God and the eternal souls of men!

In many respects, my job is not as difficult as his. I study the Word and then teach it, usually to very large

The Byesville
Alumni Banquet
is held the 1st
Saturday in June
every year.

Alma Mater

As we stand here at your portals,

Dear old Byesville High;

Singing loud your hymns of praises,

Till they reach the sky.

Hail, o hail, our alma mater,

Let the echoes ring,

Hail to thee, our alma mater,

Hail, oh hail we sing.

Evening Program

Social Hour

Registration – 5:15 – 6:15

Welcome – Judge David Cain

Pledge of Allegiance – Judge David Cain

Invocation – Judge David Cain

Dinner – 6:30pm

"Then" – Andrea Gabel

Speaker – Pastor Ken Nichols

Roll call of Classes – Judge David Cain

Oldest returning Alumni

Alumni who traveled the farthest

Tribute to deceased members – Andrea Gabel

Entertainment – Jack Short

50/50 – Money Tree – Door Prize – Gene Mills

Singing of Our Alma Mater – Judge David Cain

Dinner Menu

Salad
New York Strip Steak
Chicken Florentine
Green Bean Almandine
Buttered Parsley Redskins
Rolls and Butter
Coffee, Soda and Tea
Dessert

Alumni Committee Members

Gene Mills, Barbara Todd Robinson, Sharon Shivers, Jack Short, Andrea Degenhart Gabel, Judy Perkins Fehrman, Ron Fehrman, Sharon Siddle Zuress.

The committee wishes you an enjoyable evening with your former classmates and friends from near and far.

We would like to take this time to express our gratitude to those that have supported us or helped in any way this year.

Anniversary Years

1926	1931
1936	1941
1946	1951
1956	1961

Golden Anniversary Year is 1961.
In September 1957, 66 freshmen enrolled in
Byesville High School, in May 1961, 60 students
graduated.
Class Motto: "Not at the top, but climbing."
Class colors: Lavender and white.
Class Flower: Lavender mum.

Byesville High School was erected in 1923.
The first commencement was held May 22, 1924.
It is currently used as an elementary school for children in
Kindergarten to 5th grade in the Rolling Hills Local School District.

- Welcome -

The Annual Byesville Alumni Banquet

1924 – 1964

June 4, 2011

groups. I trust God to use His Word to change lives. Sometimes I find out what He has done. Most of the time I am left to trust the promise that His Word will not return unto Him void but will accomplish that unto which He sent it! I believe that promise and have learned to rest my case there.

But counseling is different. Thrown into life-struggles of men and women, one or two at a time, can be far more draining! When my listeners fail to really listen and choose to do nothing with my biblical counsel, I usually do not hear about it unless it results in some major failure. But biblical counselors have to face the weekly realities of unfollowed instructions and ignored advice. Frankly, I do not know how they survive. I am confident that it is not my gift! But it truly is Dr. Ken Nichols' gift. He consistently applies the truth of God's Word to the human problems of our day and prayerfully, patiently waits for God to work.

And God has worked! I could tell you the stories of many marriages that have been saved and many human souls that have been mended. Ken would be quick to say that God did it and he is correct. But perhaps you have noticed that God does some of His best work through yielded servants. I have appreciated and benefited from Ken Nichols' encouragement and wisdom for years. I have encouraged Ken to put his seminar material in writing. I teased and bugged him until he got the message and now you will get the message too.

Chapter One
FACING UP TO FEAR

So, there I was, lying on the floor of a fast-food restaurant. Two young men were busy trying to help me return to a clear conscious state. One was placing an oxygen mask over my mouth while the other was checking my heart rate with his stethoscope. You talk about fear!

I had just come from the hospital where I'd had an angiogram. That procedure had required an extended period of fasting beforehand, and apparently it's not such a good idea to break such a fast with Wendy's chili and fries. But what was really scary, even in my foggy condition, was the one EMT guy yelling at me, "Mr. Nichols, Mr. Nichols, do you know what day it is?"

I'm toast! I thought. Here I am weaving in and out of consciousness and the people who were sent to save my life don't even know what day it is! Yikes!

1

All of us experience fear. There is no escape. Things will happen in your life that cause a momentary adrenaline rush (like my fast-food crisis). This kind of fear is normal and even healthy. The problem occurs when fear piles on top of fear, when anxiety mixes in with reality, when you get used to a fear-saturated lifestyle that ties you in knots. This is all too common these days.

> Face it: The world has become a scary place. Maybe it's always been this way, but it seems that the last decade or so has amped up the fear factor.

Face it: The world has become a scary place. Maybe it's always been this way, but it seems that the last decade or so has amped up the fear factor. Each day's headlines give us new reasons to shudder. If it's not your health that's in jeopardy, it's your nest egg. If it's not the moral fabric of society, it's the air we breathe or the water we drink. Times are tough and—if you believe the host of gloomy experts spinning the stats on blogs and talk shows—times will only get tougher. The message is clear: *Be afraid; be very afraid.*

This fear does damage to us in all sorts of ways. It promotes stress, which gnaws away at our bodies. It stimulates emotional responses such as anger and depression. It strains our relationships. It challenges our faith. It can keep us from enjoying life the way we want to.

But we don't have to be all tied up in "fear-knots".

You can decide what to do with your fear. That's the message of this book. You can navigate your way through this scary world. Rather than being tied in knots by the frightening facets of life, you can meet those challenges by learning how to transform fear into faith. Or perhaps we should say, how to transform "fear knots" into "fear not's." You can redirect the energy of fear in positive directions, using it to protect yourself and others, to improve the situation, or to refocus on what's most important. One of the most terrifying things about fear is that you feel powerless, but you're not. You have the power to choose how you respond.

This is not denial. There might be some "sincerely wrong" people who suggest that the best way to face your fear is to ignore it: *Pretend there's no danger. Focus on the positive. Forget about the wild beast about to devour you; instead, admire the gleam of its teeth.*

That's not a helpful approach. It may calm you down momentarily, but it does little to change your long-term reality. In order to transform fear into faith, we need to understand it. *We can't overcome it by underestimating it.* While we don't need to be alarmist about every threat that arises, we must be realistic about the danger. Maybe some "experts" are too gloomy about the economy, the environment, or terrorism. We don't have to believe every Cassandra who prophesies doom, but we need to be informed about those situations. Some threats are real. We can't afford to close our eyes to those daunting headlines.

Swine Flu Pandemic Grows. That co-worker who's coughing—is that just a cold or something worse? This flu is especially troubling, a mutating strain that's transmitted through coughs and casual contact. Will it get worse? Will there be enough vaccine? Will it mutate into something drug-resistant? And if we weather this pandemic, what about the next one?

Economy Takes Another Tumble. The recent recession seemed to topple a house of cards. That's what made it especially scary—not that the economy took a hit, but the idea that it's been on artificial life support for some time. Will the stimulus work long-term or just saddle us with more debt? Will the economic upticks be an ongoing thing or just set us up for another collapse? Is your job safe? Will you be able to keep up with your mortgage? Is there anything left in your retirement fund?

Health Care Costs Skyrocket. If you've been following the national debate over health care, you might be sick of it, so to speak. Health insurance costs have been increasing, and insurers are becoming more finicky about the costs they'll cover. We all know of folks who got socked with unpayable medical bills because of some loophole, perhaps a "pre-existing condition." And yet we also worry that the legislative overhaul might just make things worse. Will we have to wait three years for a flu shot?

New Terrorist Attack Expected. September 11, 2001, changed America forever. We had been attacked on our own soil, and so our illusion of safety was punctured. Since then, we've learned to keep our eyes peeled for suspicious characters, to take our shoes off at airport screening checkpoints, and to worry when loved ones travel. Experts keep telling us to expect another attack sometime soon, maybe something biological or chemical. We've already seen some near-misses on flights and in big cities. And with the latest news headlines about the suspected number of "home-grown" terrorists in our country, will the next attack happen in your home town?

Rogue Nations Developing Nukes. In the 1960s, schoolchildren practiced hiding under their desks, in case of nuclear attack. It was a fearful time, but a simpler time. Only the U.S. and USSR had the bomb, and neither nation really wanted to blow up the world. In the half-century since, another dozen nations or so have developed nuclear capability or are close to it. What's more, the dismantling of the Soviet Union left the possibility that parts of their arsenal might be sold on the black market. Who has nukes and who's willing to use them?

Scientists Warn of Environmental Disasters. Decades of air and water pollution have hurt us. Scientists talk about a "global warming" in which carbon emissions have eaten away the earth's ozone layer, causing dangerous weather patterns and changes in sea level. Will your home be underwater someday, or in a desert without water?

Identity Theft on the Rise. Be careful who you hand your credit card to. Unscrupulous clerks and servers have

4

been known to steal credit card numbers. Internet pirates can hack into your computer and begin doing business in your name. Will you owe thousands you never spent? Will your credit score be ruined by someone else's prank?

Ethics Absent from Millennial Generation. What's this world coming to? Sometimes it seems that the values of previous generations have vanished. Kids are growing up these days with little sense of right and wrong. How low can we go?

Divorce Rate at an All-Time High. Not too long ago, divorce was rare and shameful. Now it's easily shrugged off, even celebrated. What will this mean for your marriage, or those of your loved ones?

Whoa! All this is enough to make you want to crawl under a rock, but there's no escaping it. Life in the 21st century is frightening. Consider how many of those fear-causing headlines are brand-new. A decade or two ago, these issues didn't exist, or they were much less of a problem. Now, each day seems to focus our attention on new fear-fueled stresses.

> These emotional ropes tie us up and rob us of our freedom to enjoy life.

These emotional ropes tie us up and rob us of our freedom to enjoy life.

What can we do? Well, it won't help to deny the factors that cause us fear. If they're real, we have to face them. And it won't help to minimize these fears, as if they're not important. Granted, some fears get pumped out of proportion by fearful imaginations, and we shouldn't over-react to those situations. But there are a number of issues that do cause us legitimate personal concern. Each of us would have a slightly different list. But here are a few to consider.

5

We are legitimately concerned about our health. We don't want to be bed-ridden with disease, and we don't want to be a burden on our families.

We are legitimately concerned about our safety. We don't want to be victims of violent crime or terrorism.

We are legitimately concerned about our way of life. Some might worry about losing money, through bank malfeasance or credit fraud, but most of us recognize it's not just about money. The money just allows us to live in a certain way, in a certain home, with a certain schedule. We don't want to be deprived of this way of life, especially if we've worked hard to attain it.

We are legitimately concerned for our loved ones. We want them to be safe and healthy, with opportunities to thrive.

So let's not deny these legitimate concerns. Let's consider carefully how to transform them from "Fear Knots" to "Fear Not's." Let's accept the fears we must face and use that energy for positive motivation, rather than harmful manipulation.

What Can We Count On?

My wife Marlene and I were spending a weekend away for rest and enjoyment. Our daughter Kendra and her husband Brad joined us in a lovely hotel on the bay in San Diego, ideal for a relaxing overnight retreat. In just a split second fear became an uninvited fifth guest of our holiday when we were awakened at 4:34 A.M. by a loud noise and the shaking of our bed.

There's a moment when you don't know what's going on. You feel the jolting effects of *something*, but you haven't identified the source—especially when it wakes you from a sound sleep. But then consciousness kicks in and you give the terror a name. *Earthquake!*

Marlene jumped out of bed and in just a few seconds was standing at the door with her jogging suit and shoes on. It took me a little longer. We were on the fourteenth floor, not a good place to be during an earthquake, and the building was still swaying back and forth. We could hear the commotion in the hall as other hotel guests screamed and ran out of their rooms, trying to get out of the building.

As it turned out, the building was a safer place than we realized. Over the next forty minutes, we joined the other guests in the hallways and lobby, expressing a full range of helplessness and fear. It seemed that everybody in the hotel was safe, including Kendra and Brad, but we began to see TV reports of injury and even death in other parts of the Northridge area. The quaking had long subsided when we finally quieted our own quaking enough to go back to bed. Then suddenly the voice of the hotel manager came over the speaker. Marlene and I jumped up again. Should we get out of the hotel? No, he was just announcing that engineers had checked the building's foundation and we had no cause to fear. (Do you suppose he actually thought that his calming comment would work?)

Later that morning we found out that the hotel was constructed with the latest state-of-the-art technology. It was mounted on rollers, which accounted for the terrifying swaying. Get this, because it gives us an important insight. Those engineers did not *deny* the power of an earthquake to shake the ground their building stood on. They didn't steel themselves against it, trying to build a structure so strong it could not be moved. They created a building that literally rolled with the punches the earth would throw. This hotel would be moved by the quake, but it would not be toppled. The devastating earthquake in Haiti provides a tragic contrast of the difference that structural design and strategic planning can make when caught in the brutality of an earthquake.

Perhaps this story can illustrate how we need to prepare for the unavoidable "emotional earthquakes" that fear can induce. We can't avoid the shaking, but we can survive it and be strengthened by it. Some might try to ignore the frightening elements of our modern world, and others might put on some kind of steely bravado, but isn't it best to just roll with the punches? Admit that you're scared, but find a way to live fully in spite of the fear. That is not as easy as it may sound.

Following the Northridge earthquake, some office workers in Southern California wore hard hats to work for several days. Many families packed their belongings—or what was left of them—and left California, not having the strength or knowledge to be set free from the bondage of fear knots that lingered in their heart and lives. Thousands of aftershocks of that disastrous quake sent people into panic. The vibrations of a low-flying jet or a ten-wheeler rumbling by would increase pulse rates, produce tears, cause clammy palms, and send schoolchildren diving under desks.

I don't blame these people. I was skittish myself. One of our most basic assumptions in life is that the ground beneath our feet is solid. We walk into a building and expect that the roof will stay above our heads. When the earth shudders, it shakes more than our bodies—it shakes our souls. If we can't trust the ground we walk on, what can we trust?

That's a good question to ask.

Another assumption that gets challenged in frightening times is this: *We are in control.* Especially in America, we like to think that we can pretty much determine our own destiny. If we work hard, invest wisely, and stay out of dangerous situations, we expect our lives to be good, healthy, productive, and pleasurable. But that's not always the case.

On September 11, 2001, all America was greeted with the news of the devastating action of terrorists who crashed jumbo jets—two into the World Trade Center, one into the Pentagon, and one that did not achieve its goal because of extremely brave passengers aboard. Thousands of innocent people were killed—passengers on the planes, workers in the buildings, fire and police personnel who had come to rescue, and passersby on the streets. Television cameras were focused on the World Trade Center when the second plane burst through the second building, increasing our horror and fear. Almost all channels covered the ongoing catastrophe, showing dust-covered survivors running in terror from collapsing buildings or jumping to their deaths from upper floors. Our nation was gripped in the kind of fear other nations have undergone for many years, but we never thought it would happen here. After all, America was isolated, cocooned, powerful, special, protected by God. Quickly, on 9-11, all our confidence was shattered.

New York City was effectively shut down for a time. Aircraft throughout the nation were grounded immediately after the horror, and people sought alternative means of travel. (Some would never again board an airplane, train, ship, or even a Greyhound bus, or take an elevator up a high-rise building, or join crowds of people at an athletic event, or shop at large shopping centers.) We Americans love our entertainment, but for the next week the only thing on TV was news related to the attacks. Day after day we saw relief workers, firefighters, and police searching for survivors in the five-story-high pile of rubble. As a nation we were collectively in shock. It was as if the very ground of our being was shaken. We experienced an earthquake at the level of the soul. Something terrible had happened that we had no control over. We had to come to grips with the thought that we were not the masters of our own fate.

It was a hard lesson to learn and an awful way to learn it, but isn't it an essential notion for us to hang onto as we go through life in the 21st century? As we sort through the terrors of modern life—economic, environmental, international, etc.—we find a number of things we have no control over. We must live with a sense of uncertainty: despite our best efforts, sometimes bad things happen.

> Denial is a bad option, but so is the other end of the spectrum. Denial says everything's fine when it isn't, but some folks anticipate disaster when everything's fine.

What If?

Denial is a bad option, but so is the other end of the spectrum. Denial says everything's fine when it isn't, but some folks anticipate disaster when everything's fine. Or they see any minor problem as a major one. It's the curse of "What if?"

What if I lose my job? What if my husband has an accident? What if my health insurance gets canceled? What if the plane crashes? What if they run out of flu vaccine and I come down with it? What if I flunk this test and can't graduate?

These people get all tied in knots by imagining crises that don't really exist. By focusing on the bad things that can happen, we begin to suffer as if those things have already happened. Rather than enjoying the reality of this moment and what is happening now, the "what if" people worry about a dismal future that might never happen.

In Shakespeare's play *Julius Caesar*, the title character refers to something that resembles the "what if" tendency:

> *Cowards die many times before their deaths;*
>
> *The valiant never taste of death but once.*
>
> *Of all the wonders that I yet have heard,*
>
> *It seems to me most strange that men should fear;*
>
> *Seeing that death, a necessary end,*
>
> *Will come when it will come.*

When people worry about dying, they die a bit. When they live in fear of what might happen, the negative results of the events they fear have already begun to affect them *even though the events haven't happened.* When you think about it, isn't that the whole point of terrorism--not just to inflict damage, but to strike terror in people's hearts about the next attack that *might* happen?

Yet, as Caesar says, death "will come when it will come." We can take reasonable precautions, but worrying about this disease or that accident doesn't help us. We need to live boldly, free of the debilitating fear of potential disaster. If those events occur, they occur, but it's senseless to let them rob us of our joy and vitality *before* they occur (if they ever do). Chronic fear and worry becomes destructive. In fact there is more emotional and physical damage from fear-induced negative anticipation than fearful realities.

- 40% of our worries are about things that never happen.
- 30% of our worries concern things that are in the past.
- 12% of our worries are needless concerns about our health.
- 10% of our worries are petty, miscellaneous worries.
- 8% of our worries are legitimate concerns.

(And frankly, even the 8% often turns out a bit better than we anticipated.)

Let's consider a frivolous example. A shy teenager named Jimmy wants to ask the lovely Brenda on a date, but he's afraid.

"What are you afraid of?" asks his best friend.

"I'm afraid she'll say no."

"So?"

"What if Brenda says she just doesn't want to go out with me? No excuse, no 'other plans.' Just 'I don't want to.' I couldn't stand that."

"Let me get this straight," the friend says. "You're afraid she won't go out with you, so you won't ask her. But if you don't ask her, that guarantees she won't go out with you. That's messed up."

"Well . . ."

"You're so afraid she'll say no, you won't give her a chance to say yes!"

11

We can see the absurdity in a hypothetical case of adolescent infatuation, but a lot of people live their lives in the same way. They fear failure, so they don't attempt to succeed. They fear disaster, so they avoid doing anything adventurous. They fear heartbreak, so they never open themselves to love.

The truth is that Brenda might say no. Jimmy might suffer disappointment. But, as his friend points out, he's allowing fear to assure a negative outcome. Some friends might decide that this is time for a pep talk: "There is no way she'll say no to you!" But that's not exactly true. There is always a chance of failure, though there's also a chance of success. Any realistic approach to life must embrace both sides of the equation. Disaster might happen, or it might not. Don't give that possibility more attention than it deserves, but don't give it too little. If we want to truly transform our fear into something positive, we can't deny the frightful things in our world, but neither can we obsess about them.

A fear-drenched preoccupation with the past and paranoia about the future can cause paralysis in the present. And often that paralysis keeps you from counter-acting the future events you dread. Some would say that your fears *bring about* the negative outcomes. Sometimes that's true, as in the case of Jimmy, but other times our fearful paralysis just makes it difficult to prepare for or adjust to those unwanted events.

Fear to Faith

Not long ago, my wife, Marlene, and I moved across the country, from San Diego to Virginia. This was not a good time to move. The national economy was in a free fall and a mortgage crisis dominated the headlines. Marlene was especially fretful about all the details of this complicated journey—selling our house, buying a new one in unfamiliar territory, and of course the sorting, pitching and packing that always accompanies a major move.

But rather than letting fear paralyze her, she let it prod her into a deeper experience of faith. Claiming the Bible verses, "You do not have because you do not ask" (James 4:2 NKJV) and "He who calls you is faithful, who also will do it." (1 Thessalonians 5:24). She began praying specifically that the Lord would provide for us in unexpected ways during the uncertain days ahead. The faith of those prayers began to untie her fear knots. She had a new confidence about the move, trusting that God would guide the process in ways she couldn't predict.

A few days later, Marlene opened our mail to receive a delightful surprise, a notice from a financial corporation. Many years earlier, she had taken out an annuity but for some reason had not received yearly statements about the account. She had completely forgotten about this interest-bearing account. And now, just when we were stretched as tight as could be, she received this timely reminder, a personal answer from the Lord that He was in control of our circumstances.

I am sure there are reasonable explanations for why the company did not send us any notices for almost fifteen years, that we "just happened" to have lost track of it in our own financial plan. But Marlene and I are thoroughly convinced that God was answering her prayer by specifically providing for us in an unexpected way—thus using this anxious time in our lives to grow our faith.

The emotion of fear itself is not the problem. It's what we do with it. Will we redirect its power or let it tie us in knots? When fear restrains us, it saps our energy and ensures disaster. But when we understand fear and respond with spiritual strength and personal wisdom, we can untie those knots, gain freedom from fear's control and enjoy the journey of life, even when experiencing the emotional earthquakes that are unavoidable along the way.

Personal Evaluation

1. How have current world conditions interfered with your ability to do your work or enjoy your life? Do you have physical, emotional, spiritual or relational problems that you attribute to the effects of fear?

_____

_____

_____

_____

_____

_____

_____

_____

_____

_____

_____

_____

_____

2. Which of the following approaches do you usually take:

   * Denying the realities that would frighten you;

   * Worrying about "what if's" that might never happen;

   * Actively and intentionally confronting your fears?

3. What specific attitudes and behaviors could you implement to untie the fear knots in your life?

_____

_____

_____

_____

_____

_____

_____

_____

_____

_____

4. If you were helping someone else facing fears, what would you suggest to them in terms of their spiritual life? How has unwanted fear impacted your spiritual health?

_____

_____

_____

_____

_____

_____

_____

_____

Practical Application

1. List five "what-ifs" that invade your thinking. Then rate them 1-10 as to how probable each one is to happen. At least consider "what if" they do happen? Then what?

   a. _____

   b. _____

   c. _____

   d. _____

   e. _____

2. Rate the following according to this question: *Does it make me more fearful or less fearful?* Put a plus sign beside those that make you more fearful, and a minus sign beside those that calm your fears. (Put two signs if it has an extreme effect either way.)

__ TV News	__ Talk Radio	__ Church Attendance
__ Internet Blogs	__ Family Conversations	__ Talk with Co-workers
— Praying	— Shopping	— Going on Vacation
__ Facebook or Twitter	__ Watching a Movie	__ Trying New Experiences

Prayerful Meditation

1. **Fear Not**—God knows about what is ahead in your life and you can trust him to give you a steadfast heart.

   "You will have no fear of bad news; your heart is steadfast, trusting in the Lord" (Psalms 112:7).

2. **Fear Not**—God is never preoccupied or distracted from hearing our cries for help.

   "The righteous cry out, and the Lord hears them; he delivers them from all their troubles" (Psalms 34:17).

3. **Fear Not**—The Lord Jesus stands ready to protect and encourage you. He will untie the fear knots in your heart and give to you perfect peace.

   "And the peace of God, which transcends all understanding, will guard your hearts and your minds in Christ Jesus" (Philippians 4:7).

Chapter Two
UNTYING

When I was a young lad,
I was a proud Boy Scout. I wasn't in the program for long, but one thing I remember clearly was learning how to tie knots. There were many different ways to tie a knot, depending on what purpose you had in mind. And they were all untied in unique ways. One knot would be untied with just a tug on one end. Another required a near-surgical operation of twists and turns.

I suppose we can find a lesson there about fear. God often allows us to experience fearful situations in our lives for a very specific purpose. Sometimes, to our amazement, these "fear knots" can be quickly resolved, but others are complex, requiring a lot of prayer and patience before we're set free from emotional bondage. We need to understand that fear has its purpose in our lives--for example, building personal character and spiritual strength—and we need to anticipate some complexity in unraveling that fear.

It's not simply a question of "to fear or not to fear." We don't need to banish fear from our lives entirely. That would be utter denial. We need to study our fear, depend on a growing faith to untie those strands, and avoid bondage to it.

Fearless Heroes

Sometimes we get the idea that we need to be like the action heroes we see in the movies. Those guys seem fearless, don't they? Hollywood has made a specialty of the wise-cracking swashbuckler, the irreverent hero who laughs in the face of doom. The story always seems to come down to some critical moment when Bruce Willis or Will Smith or Christian Bale [or insert your own actor] jumps out of the plane or runs into the burning building or disarms the nuke [or insert your own valiant deed] in order to save the world or the president or the pretty girl [choose one].

But are we really supposed to believe that these heroes don't care about the danger? It would be foolish to face such cataclysmic situations without a sense of how serious they are. True courage is not the absence of fear, but the willingness to do what needs to be done in spite of the terrifying circumstances.

I once had my own Hollywood-style adventure. It was six weeks after my truck had been stolen. I stopped at the 7-11 for a morning coffee and there it was, my missing truck, parked right in front of the store! I saw the young (and very big) man who had been driving it. He was now inside the store, buying his coffee. This was my chance. I sprang into action.

Let me pause here to note that it can be very dangerous to be a 60-year-old former paratrooper like me. I still have the spirit, but not the body. That is a high-risk combination. So, in my attempt to imitate a cinematic action hero, I ran up to the truck thief, grabbed the keys out of his hands, and yelled at the store clerk to call 911. He was no pushover. Pushing me back, he wrestled the keys out of my hands and ran to the truck. He got the door locked before I could get there. I pulled my arm back and with the palm of my hand hit the window with all my strength.

Here is the way I envisioned the story turning out. The window would smash, I would biff the thief and grab the keys, just in time for the cops to show up and arrest him. I had seen such drama work out that way in the movies.

In reality, I nearly broke my hand. The tires screeched as he backed out of the parking lot. I ran down the street and jumped in front of the truck (not a particularly bright move on my part), thinking he would not want to run over me and then I would have another chance to get my truck back. He actually hit the accelerator! I hit the hood of the truck with my hands and pushed myself out of the way. He took off and I was ramped up with so much fear-induced adrenaline I was shaking. And unlike the Hollywood version of my story, this would-be hero did not save the day or get his truck back.

I know, I know, it's not a good idea to base your life on Hollywood films. That's why I was interested to read a news story online about heroes from World War II. Researcher Brian Wansink of Cornell University interviewed hundreds of veterans to see what they thought about heroism. It turns out that loyalty was more important to these soldiers than bravado. "You show me a man who says he was brave over there, and I'll show you a liar," says one Bronze Star recipient. "Every one of us was afraid. Even the Germans were afraid." [NOTE 1]

So these real-life heroes weren't laughing in the face of danger, but they persevered through it. Why? Because they believed in something more important—loyalty to their company, allegiance to their nation, and for many, faith in their God.

We find something similar in the New Testament book of Hebrews. One chapter goes through a list of Old Testament heroes—Abraham, Sarah, Moses, David, and so on—commenting on the faith that made them do what they did. The chapter ends with a catch-all honor roll of anonymous heroes who "conquered kingdoms, administered justice, . . . shut the mouths of lions, quenched the fury of the flames, and escaped the edge of the sword; whose weakness was turned to strength, . . . were tortured, . . . faced jeers and flogging, . . . put in prison, . . . were stoned, . . . sawed in two, . . . put to death by the sword, . . . destitute, persecuted and mistreated" (Hebrews 11:33-37).

Were these folks somehow immune from the terror of these ordeals? I doubt it. Were they afraid? Probably. But they moved forward through faith. As Hebrews puts it, "their weakness was turned to strength."

So as you find your own opportunity for fear-conquering heroism, what will it look like? Will you fight your way through a tough economy to provide for your family? Will you risk your health to care for a sick friend? Will you demonstrate hope and joy in your life despite a world gone awry? You might do any of these things, but the question remains: In order to practice "heroism" in our modern world, do you have to be free of all fear? No. You might be scared silly as you face the challenges of modern life. Just don't let fear tie you up in emotional knots that keep you from doing what needs to be done.

Two Kinds of Fear

A friend tells of a childhood incident that could have turned tragic, but he can laugh about it now. When he was about 12, he joined his older brother and a friend in a summer business mowing lawns in the neighborhood. Even at that age, he had plenty of experience mowing his own lawn, and he could be trusted to work responsibly and safely. But one client wanted these boys to use his own power mower. My friend wasn't familiar with this sort of machine, which could basically push itself—the operator just needed to steer it, or stop it. At his age, he was still rather small and not very strong, so when he started up the mower, it was all he could do to keep up, and unfortunately he couldn't turn it before it took out a section of the client's garden.

That story makes me think of fear. The question we've been considering is this: *Are you managing it, or is it manipulating you?* Far too many people are like my friend with the power mower. Their fear is pulling them along where they don't want to go, and doing damage in the process. How can we grab hold of this powerful force and make it work for us?

Fear is part of the emotional equipment given to us at birth— even before birth, for babies in the womb have been known to jump at a loud sound. Many fears are positive and productive because they prod us to do something about fearful situations. Fear is healthy and helpful when you step off a curb, hear a loud honk and jump back just as a car screeches by. It's fear that prompted you to get out of the way. Do parents want their children to fear the cars that go roaring past on the street? Absolutely. Nobody wants an overly timid child, but a healthy fear of a speeding automobile can literally be a life-saver.

Fear keeps you from touching a hot stove, walking too near a cliff edge, or turning the wrong way on a one-way street. In moments of danger, fear can be a powerful motivator, activating your sense of self-preservation and survival as it pumps adrenaline into your bloodstream, allowing you to face impending danger with courage and confidence.

> Fear keeps you from touching a hot stove, walking too near a cliff edge, or turning the wrong way on a one-way street.

This motivating fear causes a husband to walk five days in the snow to get help for his stranded family. It gives a young mother strength to lift a crashed car off her toddler's leg. Motivating fear is a positive force.

But there's a big difference between this motivating fear and what we might call "manipulating fear." Think about the instance we just mentioned: jumping out of the way of a speeding car. In the following minutes, your heart pounds and pulse races. All your senses are on high alert. The car is far down the road by now, but you're still reacting to the danger.

Have you ever loaded a computer program and then changed your mind? You want to cancel that program and start another, but you have to wait for the first program to finish loading before you can exit out of it. This might not apply if you have a super-fast computer, but the principle is there. You have started a program that needs to run its course before you exit from it. Your physical response to fear is much the same. Your body goes on high alert, and then the danger passes, but it takes a few minutes for you to calm down. In fact, you might still be jumpy a few hours later. You might even have a nightmare about it. But eventually the reaction passes and your systems get back to normal.

What if you don't get back to normal? What if you remain so terrified of passing cars that you never want to cross the street again? That could be a problem. You hear a car revving in the distance and already your palms sweat, your heart pounds. You set a foot on the asphalt and you look both ways, and you look both ways again, and you can't step any farther. You keep imagining a car racing toward you. You're frozen there, helpless, paralyzed.

In essence, the "fear program" is still running in your system. You can't exit. This is what phobias are about. I know a man who, when he was eight, was held underwater by rambunctious playmates, and he hasn't gone swimming since. He's now eighty. He experienced a powerful trauma back then, a fear that he would drown, and that fear has affected his life for seven-some decades. I don't mean to make light of that fear. I can only imagine how terrible it must have been for him as a child. But that fear should have subsided in time. Instead, the fear program kicks on again whenever he goes to the beach. Rationally, he knows that it won't happen again. He's with friends and family who wouldn't dream of hurting him. But he focuses on the fear of the past, and it paralyzes him in the present.

Remember the anthrax scare of 2001? In the months after the 9/11 attacks, the nation was already on alert. Isolated cases of anthrax spores enclosed in a few letters sent the entire nation into terror. People ironed their mail or put it in their microwave ovens before opening it, or refused to open it altogether. Postal workers started wearing gloves and masks. When a staff member to Senate Majority Leader Tom Daschle opened a letter laced with anthrax spores, exposing twenty-one people, panic set in. Although the Senate stayed open, the House shut down. As one newsweekly put it, "Terrorism had done what a civil war could not—halt the legislative arm of our democracy."[NOTE 2]

Anyone living near a suspect area ran to the doctor with the least symptom of what could have been anthrax. In response, Bob Chapman, a former Pentagon official said, "If the weapon is fear, and I think it is, it's the terror in terrorism that is the weapon."[NOTE 3]

Here again, we find examples of both a healthy motivating fear and an unhealthy manipulating fear. Without a doubt, many millions of people believed they were facing dangerous circumstances, and they took certain measures to protect themselves. But which measures were wise and which were foolish? Which were based on a rational appraisal of the risk, and which were results of an irrational sense of panic?

One lesson we learn from the anthrax crisis is that *fear piles up*. The reaction would have been much different in 2005 or 1995, but immediately after the 9/11 attacks, our fear program was already running. We were primed to be afraid of *something*, and the anthrax scare filled that negative anticipation.

Adding to the problem is another factor: *fear is contagious.* Even if you're not overly fearful about a situation, it just takes a conversation or two with a terrified friend to shiver your timbers. Some people seem to feel it's their duty to alert everyone around them to the real or imagined dangers that lurk around every corner. If you're not as fearful as they are, you're just not being responsible. Or so they say.

The flames of fear often get fanned by the media. "Something in your house could be killing you! Details at eleven." How often do you hear those prime-time teasers? Fear sells. Broadcasters know you'll tune in and stay tuned if you think your safety is on the line. In addition, a number of media celebs thrive on pushing their political platforms by stirring fear about the opposition. "If [fill in the *other* political party] gets its way, it will mean the end of civilization as we know it."

In all these ways, we can find our healthy *motivating* fear getting morphed into an unhealthy *manipulating* fear. I find a great example of that in a story from the New Testament about Jesus' disciples.

> The flames of fear often get fanned by the media. "Something in your house could be killing you! Details at eleven."

Crossing the Sea of Galilee by boat, with Jesus asleep in the stern, they encountered a storm of great intensity. Now several of these disciples were experienced fishermen who had sailed this sea often, but this was apparently the worst tempest they had ever known.

Motivating fear led them to do all they could to save the boat—and their own lives. They would have turned the boat into the wind, furiously bailed out water, and tossed overboard all non-essential tackle and cargo. Yet, after they had exhausted all their efforts to save themselves, the storm still raged and the little boat still tossed and bucked in the wild waves. The fury of the storm so dominated the proud fishermen's hearts that they held little hope of outlasting the angry waves and roaring wind. Motivating fear had become manipulative. Their hearts were tied in knots.

But Jesus slept through all this. In desperation, the disciples shook him awake and shouted, "Teacher, don't you care if we drown?"

Jesus got up and spoke directly to the wind and waves. "Quiet! Be still!" When the wind died down and the sea was completely calm, Jesus then asked his disciples, "Why are you so afraid? Do you still have no faith?" (Mark 4:35-41).

The disciples had started out by trusting their own ability to weather the storm. They were alert to the danger and took steps to protect themselves. When the storm proved too great for them, manipulating fear kicked in. They began to doubt everything, even the power and love of the Lord. *Don't you care if we drown?* Of course he cared, and he proved it in awesome fashion.

What can we learn here? As our motivating fear turns into manipulating fear, how can we move in the direction of faith? Well, just as there are different kinds of fear, we might also talk about different kinds of faith.

Fear Grows Faith

Sometimes, when people urge faith in the face of fear, they're really talking about *denial*. "Everything will be all right. Nothing will go wrong. You'll be fine. Don't worry."

In some cases, this is true. When our fears get whipped up to unreasonable levels, we need sensible reassurance. Often, after hearing of a high-profile plane crash, people are afraid to fly. A friend might say, "Actually, flying is still safer than driving," and they'd be right. (That might then make you afraid to *drive*, but they mean well.)

Yet there are many times when people offer false reassurance. Say a person faces a dangerous surgery, with a 50-50 chance of survival. A loved one might say, "You'll be fine. It's a piece of cake. There's no way anything bad will happen!" They might mean well, but this is not really true. They might call it positive thinking, but it's actually denial. And this is what a lot of people think of when they hear the word *faith*. Optimism. Assuming the best outcome, even if the facts say otherwise.

The "faith" of denial is irresponsible, and it often backfires. In an effort to calm the *manipulating* fear, which could be destructive, these well-wishers take away *motivating* fear, which could be helpful. If I'm facing a dangerous surgery, I want to know exactly what the chances are. I want to be prepared for any outcome. If I have to drive on icy roads, don't tell me the weather's fine. I want to know exactly how hazardous conditions are, so I can drive accordingly.

Denial often backfires because we know better. When people paint too rosy a picture, when we know it's a dangerous situation, we begin to worry, "What aren't they telling us?" As long as we're kept in the dark about the true situation, those fears can quickly become manipulative.

> Yet real faith is more than positive thinking. It's a trust in purpose. It's not a blind assurance that nothing can go wrong. It's an assurance that there is a purpose behind whatever happens.

In our current national crises, you might hear people say, "Don't worry! We won't see another terrorist attack." Or, "You won't catch the H1N1 virus." Or, "No problem. I'm sure your investments are fine." That might be positive thinking, but none of those statements are certain truths. If we allow ourselves to experience *motivating* fear, without being paralyzed by *manipulative* fear, we can take the necessary precautions.

Yet real faith is more than positive thinking. It's a trust in *purpose*. It's not a blind assurance that nothing can go wrong. It's an assurance that there is a purpose behind whatever happens.

Of course I'm talking about *God's* purpose, but I want to be careful how we talk about this. You see, there are many people who talk about faith in God, but they're really pushing a form of denial. "God would never let any harm come to

28

you," they might say. Is that true? No! Harm often comes to believers. Ten of the original apostles were brutally killed because of their faith. Believers suffer sickness and injury just like everyone else. "God will make everything all right," people might say, but it depends on how you define "all right."

Some folks like to quote a Bible verse--Romans 8:28. This verse is precious to me, so I'm not mocking it, but I think it often gets misused. "And we know that all things work together for good . . . ." When you're facing a potentially harmful situation, someone might say, "Cheer up! It will all work together for good." Does that mean the problem will vanish if you have enough faith? No.

Consider what the whole verse says: "And we know that all things work together for good, for those who love him *and are called according to his purpose.*" So, what's this "good" that everything is leading toward? It's not a pain-free, harm-free, danger-free existence. It's an existence that goes according to God's purpose. Whatever the outcome, it will not be meaningless.

How Then?

So how will we transform fear into faith? How can we get set free from the bondage of the FEAR KNOTS and embrace the truth of God's FEAR NOTS? The rest of this book will dig into the details, but here's the short answer:

- Remember that there are two kinds of fear. On the one hand, there's a motivating fear that alerts us to danger and calls us to action. On the other hand, there's a manipulating fear that alarms us and paralyzes us.

- Note also that there are two kinds of faith. There's a kind of "positive thinking" that's based on personal confidence and general optimism. This can some-

29

times get us through hard times, but it tends to vanish when we need it most. The second kind of faith is the more powerful, because it's based on a relationship with the living God and a trust in his promises.

Personal Evaluation

1. Is fear piling onto previous fear? Are you listening too much to fearmongers in your community or in the media? Is the fear becoming irrational?

   _____

   _____

2. If you've been practicing denial, or hearing it from well-meaning friends, try to steer yourself back to rationality. What are the potential outcomes, and what are the chances? Take an honest look at what you're dealing with and then factor in God's divine purpose. Has he placed you in a "faith" workshop, entitled Fear 101? You might want to spend some serious time talking with God about this. In the language of the last part of Romans 8:28, what purpose has he "called" you to? This is the faith that will strengthen you in frightful times.

   _____

   _____

   _____

   _____

   _____

   _____

3. Is there anything you refuse to do because of the potential danger it may entail? (Perhaps you still refuse to fly anywhere.) Is this a reasonable caution or a needless phobia? Where does it come from?

_____

_____

_____

_____

_____

_____

_____

_____

4. If you have children, have you talked with them to find out what kind of fears they are facing? Fear in children, like adults, presents a great faith-building, teaching opportunity.

_____

_____

_____

_____

_____

_____

_____

_____

_____

31

Practical Application

1. Read Psalm 91 *(on right page)* every day for a week. Post a copy on your refrigerator, on your bed stand, or in your car. Believe that God has not changed. He will guard you just as he did the psalmist.

2. Write a description of a fear you may be dealing with. Begin to think how you can defeat this fear by understanding it, praying about it, and believing that God can untie the knot and set you free from its control of you as you surrender it to him.

_____

_____

_____

_____

_____

_____

_____

_____

_____

_____

_____

_____

3. Memorize 2 Timothy 1:7: "For God did not give us a spirit of timidity, but a spirit of power, of love and of self- discipline." Strive for this balance of power, love, and self-discipline in areas in your life that need to change and grow.

Prayerful Meditation

He who dwells in the shelter of the Most High

    will rest in the shadow of the Almighty.

I will say of the Lord, "He is my refuge and my fortress,

    my God, in whom I trust."

Surely he will save you from the fowler's snare

    and from the deadly pestilence.

He will cover you with his feathers,

    and under his wings you will find refuge;

    his faithfulness will be your shield and rampart.

You will not fear the terror of night,

    nor the arrow that flies by day,

nor the pestilence that stalks in the darkness,

    nor the plague that destroys at midday.

A thousand may fall at your side,

    ten thousand at your right hand,

    but it will not come near you.

You will only observe with your eyes

    and see the punishment of the wicked.

If you make the Most High your dwelling—

    even the Lord, who is my refuge—

Then no harm will befall you,

    no disaster will come near your tent.

For he will command his angels concerning you

    to guard you in all your ways;

they will lift you up in their hands,

    so that you will not strike your foot against a stone.

You will tread upon the lion and the cobra;

    You will trample the great lion and the serpent.

"Because he loves me," says the Lord, "I will rescue him;

I will protect him, for he acknowledges my name.

He will call upon me, and I will answer him;

I will deliver him and honor him.

With long life will I satisfy him

and show him my salvation.

(Psalm 91)

Chapter Three
FEARTHINK
How Your Thoughts Get Twisted

The envelope looked menacing from the start. A registered letter from the Indiana State Board of Licensing. Working as a state-certified psychologist, I needed that licensing. After signing for it, I tore open that envelope.

The letter read something like this:

Dear Dr. Nichols:

It has come to our attention that you may be in violation of rule number . . . and code number . . . of the Indiana Mental Health Professional Bureau. Individuals in violation of these statutes may receive fines, disciplinary action or the loss of license. Please be in contact with the State Board at your earliest convenience.

35

My adrenaline began to surge. I could feel the emotional ropes of fear tightening around my heart. *What was going on here?* My thoughts bounced through every aspect of my work, making it hard to focus. My counseling ministry had carefully followed professional guidelines, as far as I knew. I mentally reviewed our procedures and practice in the local church setting and could identify no glitches. Still, my mind began assembling a worst-case scenario: *I will be fined, lose my license, be subject to professional discipline and greatly embarrass the church, my family, and myself!*

That night, sleepless and nauseated, I continued to grapple with the "what-ifs" of my situation. *Will this hit the local papers? What will my friends say, or my professional colleagues? What about all the people I've counseled—will they get discouraged, or angry with me?* It was as though the power of fear came in and romped through my body and mind without restraint.

Other than that, I think I handled it quite well.

In the morning, exhausted and very much in the grip of manipulating fear, I began to develop a plan to get free from my anxiety and clear up my distorted thinking. The first order of business was to call the board. With some lingering fear I tapped out the number of the State Board. With a dry throat and a wimpy voice, I introduced myself and referred to the intimidating letter. Then I began to explain the professional procedures our ministry had been following faithfully, trying to sound strong and confident but sure I was failing miserably. When I had said everything I needed to say, I stopped . . . and waited . . . listening for the man's reply.

The silence seemed to last a lifetime. I could hear him shuffling papers and typing on the keyboard. He cleared his throat and then said, "Oops!" The man on the phone casually explained that they had overlooked the fact that we were a non-profit religious organization. Slightly different rules applied. Now that he saw that, he affirmed that we had indeed established our counseling ministry with appropriate professional guidelines. I was momentarily tempted to trade in my fear for a goodly portion of anger, but decided otherwise.

Whew! Crisis averted. We were fine.

We had always been fine. I *knew* we had followed the official guidelines. It was merely an administrative oversight, something that was easily cleared up with a phone call.

So why had I let it tie me in knots for such a long time?

I did what many people do. I received some bad news and I let my fear enlarge it into *terrible* news. My mind quickly manufactured a worst-case scenario and then acted as if that had already happened.

> Fear distorts our thinking, so that reasonable concerns are expanded into irrational terror. This leads us to make bad choices, which can worsen the original situation, or perhaps keep us from improving it.

Fact: The licensing board was questioning my procedures.

Fear-induced Fantasy: This could be an absolutely awful experience, destroying my reputation and my livelihood.

Unharnessed fear drove me rapidly from fact to fantasy. In the process, it kept me (at least temporarily) from dealing properly with the original fact. It almost kept me from picking up that phone. Imagine what would have happened if I was too afraid to call the board? My fear would have needlessly created the very situation I was afraid of.

That happens a lot. Fear distorts our thinking, so that reasonable concerns are expanded into irrational terror. This leads us to make bad choices, which can worsen the original situation, or perhaps keep us from improving it.

The Two Circles

You might think of this situation as two circles, your Circle of Concern and your Circle of Control. The Circle of Concern includes all the things that we care about—job issues, family crises, financial worries, national events. People spend a lot of time fretting about the items in this larger circle, but it's really pointless to do so, because they have no control over those situations. I love the comment Jesus made about this. "Who . . . by worrying can add a single hour to his life?" (Matthew 6:29). The fact is, we *subtract* hours from our lives with the stress of worrying and the toll that it takes on our bodies.

Does this mean we must take an apathetic, fatalistic approach—"whatever will be, will be"? Not at all, because there's another circle there. Some of the things we're concerned about we *do* have some measure of control over. We can improve relationships, save money, or change jobs. These tactics aren't always easy, but they could change things for the better. And, rather than wasting time and energy worrying about everything in the larger Circle of Concern, it makes far more sense to find those things in our Circle of Control and apply our efforts to them.

You're probably familiar with the Serenity Prayer:

God, grant me the serenity
To accept the things I cannot change;
The courage to change the things that I can;
And the wisdom to know the difference.

This familiar prayer is all about the two circles. If we take it in backwards order, the first step in confronting our fears is to apply wisdom in sorting out what we can change and what we can't. In other words, we're dividing up our concerns between the two circles. When I got that frightening letter from the State Board, the first thing I needed to do was to call and get more information so I could sort things out. Which I did . . .

eventually. In that case I didn't need to do much, just alert them to their goof. In another situation, maybe I'd need to fill out a form or change a policy, and that would fix the problem. The point is, there are often things you can do—things within your Circle of Control—to ease the situation. Those issues that fall into the Circle of Concern—"the things you cannot change"—are outside of your control, and all your worrying won't help. The best solution for those matters is to pray—both because God grants us serenity and because he is capable of changing things that we can't.

> A preoccupation with "what ifs" can quickly lead us into irrational thinking. Fear piles on top of fear, convincing you that your worst-case scenario, no matter how unlikely, will play out.

A preoccupation with "what ifs" can quickly lead us into irrational thinking. Fear piles on top of fear, convincing you that your worst-case scenario, no matter how unlikely, will play out.

I heard of one lady who was driving her husband crazy with a particular phobia. Whenever they went out, about ten minutes into their trip, she would express her fear that she had left the iron on and the house would burn down. Despite his protests, she would insist he turn the car around and go back home to check. Understandably, it became a major source of conflict in their marriage. So one time they were running a bit late for an appointment and, ten minutes from home, the wife grabbed her husband's arm and exclaimed, "Honey, I left the iron on!" He didn't get upset this time, but veered quickly into a gas station. She was surprised and pleased, assuming he was turning around to save the house from potential destruction. Instead, he stopped the car, removed the keys from the ignition, ran around to the rear of the car, popped the trunk, triumphantly lifted out the iron and handed it to his wife. Without another word they continued on to their destination.

Well, that's one way to move something from the Circle of Concern to the Circle of Control. I don't mean to make light of obsessions and phobias. Occasionally these are deep-rooted problems that require therapy. But sometimes they can be tamed with wisdom. Figure out something you can do to ease the situation, and do that.

> "More important than the circumstances in life is your response to them." How you respond will either tighten the fear knots around your heart or refocus your attention on the fear not's of God's promises. You choose.

Are you haunted by the distortions of fear-induced worries? Learn to sort through these matters. Wisely prepare for certain possibilities, and pray about those dangers that are out of your control. In my conference ministry I often make this statement: "More important than the circumstances in life is your response to them." How you respond will either tighten the fear knots around your heart or refocus your attention on the fear not's of God's promises. You choose.

Dread of the Future

Negative anticipation of a future experience is often greater than the experience itself. In some cases, the anticipation can be even more damaging.

When Cindy, a college student, lost her father to cancer, she began to experience an uncontrollable fear of premature death. She got into a habit of constantly monitoring her body symptoms and making excessive trips to doctors' offices, convinced that some disease was quietly preparing to snuff out her life.

This is not uncommon. I can personally relate to the dangers of such negative anticipation. My brother Larry, who is only one year older than me, had a mild heart attack a few years ago. He had to be in the hospital for angioplasty, was given a special diet, and is now on medication. My father had a major heart problem a year later. He too had to be hospitalized to have his arteries cleaned out. All three of my mother's brothers died of heart-related diseases. With that kind of family history it would be easy for me to become morbidly preoccupied with every heartbeat. After all, I am a Type-A personality, and I love chips and salsa.

But here's the problem. I could actually experience more physical and emotional damage from negative anticipation than I might ever experience with actual heart problems. Sure, it makes sense to live wisely within my Circle of Control, but it's counterproductive to become obsessed with the threat of death. We all will die. But to fear death every day of our lives causes us to lose out on the joys available to us while we are here on earth.

Someone like Cindy, whose life becomes dominated by the fear of death, in a way has died already. As she frets about every phantom symptom, she is missing out on the thrill of living. I feel the same way about those who are "sure" that another terrorist attack will destroy life as we know it, or that disease will run rampant, or that the environment will turn on us, or the economy will collapse. I'm not saying that everything will always be hunky-dory, but when we dwell on these fears, we are already acting as if the worst has happened. *If fear drives you into a bomb shelter in your home—or in your heart—you are doing as much damage to your life as any external attack would, maybe more.*

> If fear drives you into a bomb shelter in your home—or in your heart—you are doing as much damage to your life as any external attack would, maybe more.

Jesus talked about living an "abundant life," or as more modern translations put it, "life to the full" or "in all its fullness" (John 10:10). That's what I want, for myself and for you. So, yes, I'll get regular checkups and try to adopt a heart-healthy lifestyle, but I won't stop living simply because I'm afraid I might . . . stop living. That would make no sense at all.

Media Saturation

Remember Y2K? Many of us were preparing for the worst. Amazingly, as 1999 rolled into 2000, experts didn't know what the millions of computers in the world would do. Since their inception, these machines had been reading years as two digits, not four, so the new millennium was expected to confound them. Since so much of our existence is controlled by computers, many commentators expected life as we know it to stop short. Financial markets down. Utility grids frozen. Cars disabled. All summer and fall we heard about the impending disaster. People were gathering survival kits—canned goods, bottled water, shotguns—just in case. Our hearts were beating a lot faster during the countdown to 2000. Five, four, three, two, one . . .

And nothing happened.

More precisely, *everything* happened, just as it always had. The lights stayed on. Machines were working as before. Our cars started up. Our computers logged on to the Internet. We were just fine.

Why were we so worried about Y2K? For most of us, the problem was something we knew nothing about. We relied on the opinions of "experts," and the mass media provided a steady stream of them. And what kind of expert do they like most? The kind that tells us something big and bad is going to happen. That's how they get us to tune in. That's how they sell papers. You're not going to hear: "Everything's fine. Details at eleven."

No! They will grab us by scaring us.

Linda, a member of my church, realized that media reports were stoking her stress—and she decided to do something about it. She began to limit her exposure to news programs, especially magazine shows that focused on heinous crimes. Oh, she got enough news to be a well-informed citizen, but she didn't dwell on repetitive accounts of the terrifying or gruesome details.

A new problem emerged for Linda: her mom. Knowing that her daughter now had minimal exposure to television, Linda's mother took it upon herself to keep her up to date on all the bad news. She didn't mean any harm, but she would quickly launch into conversations about, say, the women in nearby neighborhoods that had been raped, liquor stores that had been robbed, children molested, and so on. As you might guess, this caused a problem for Linda.

Up to this point, Linda had been managing the Circles of Concern and Control quite well. Realizing that she *could* do little about the frightening events in the world around her, she focused on something she could control, her exposure to the news. But now there was a new challenge. Her well-intentioned mother was sabotaging Linda's well-designed plan. You might be thinking, *Why couldn't she just ask her mother not to tell her these things?* Well, there's one thing I haven't told you yet about Linda: *she had a deep-seated fear of confrontation.* Especially with her mom.

So suddenly the Circle of Concern wasn't just out there in the big wide world. It was personal. She could turn off the news, but she couldn't stop listening to her mom, could she? As Linda saw it, there was nothing she could do. She was doomed to be stressed out by a terrifying world, with her mother constantly turning up the heat.

But with the help of a counselor, Linda began to seize control of her situation. She *did* have some power with her mother, and she needed to exert it. Mustering all the courage she had, Linda graciously confronted her mom, and it went exactly as she expected. Badly. Mom always had to be right. Any mention of the boundaries Linda had to set up for herself was swiftly dismissed. To her credit, Linda held her ground, and it was exhausting. Finally she said, "Mom, I love you very much, but the next time you begin describing things that affect me negatively, I will have to end our conversation by leaving the room or hanging up the phone."

This conversation was a tremendous victory for Linda, because she realized she was no longer powerless. She had pulled this whole matter—not only the media issue but her relationship with her mother—into her Circle of Control. Still, I had to wonder how things went after that. Did she stick to her guns?

"I only had to walk out of the room once," she reported later with a triumphant smile. "Mom and I met at a restaurant to have lunch. We were just finishing when she began [to talk about the news]. I opened my purse, put down money on the table to cover both of our meals, gave her a kiss on the cheek, and said, 'I enjoyed our time together so much, Mom, and I want to make sure I have a sweet memory about it later—I've got to go.'"

What Others Think

In Linda's case we saw another fear besides just a dread of the future, something more personal and often more challenging—a fear of what others think. Day by day, in the minutia of our lives, this fear probably affects us more than any other. *What will people say? How will they react? What if someone objects?*

Sometimes these fears are focused on particular people in our lives—for Linda, it was her mom—and sometimes we live in fear of offending a vague, faceless "they." You know: *They* say you shouldn't wear white after Labor Day; *they* say you should be married by the time you're 30; *they* say certain opinions are old-fashioned. Either way, this fear keeps us from being ourselves. We are held back from living the way we want because we worry about the potential disapproval of others. This is one of the most complex fear knots to untie.

I'm not saying we should *try* to offend people. I'm not even saying we shouldn't care what others think. It's an important part of maturity to be aware of your effect on others. And there are situations where you *need* approval from some sort of authority figure, so it's a good idea to care what that person thinks of you. But too many of us live our whole lives this way.

This is distorted thinking. *Fear can inflate our need for approval to a point where it becomes pre-eminent, exceeding our need to pursue success, express creativity, or grow spiritually.* "But it would just be the worst thing if people were offended!" you might be thinking. That's fear talking, twisting the truth. Offending people is not the worst thing. The worst thing might be a life that was never fully lived because of this fear.

In extreme cases, this fear of disapproval takes the form of perfectionism. People brutally drive themselves toward success because they're afraid to fail. Failure would be an embarrassment, a disgrace. Often this attitude is instilled in kids by overly demanding parents, and well into adulthood the children maintain this fear of letting their parents down. We often see the success stories that result from this treatment--gifted athletes at the top of their game—but we seldom see the dark side. In his autobiography, tennis star Andre Agassi tells of the demands his father placed on him as a child, to the point that he hated the sport he excelled at. Driven by a fear of coming in second, he gained success, but he lost the joy of life along the way.

> Fear can inflate our need for approval to a point where it becomes pre-eminent, exceeding our need to pursue success, express creativity, or grow spiritually.

Too many parents pass on this distorted, fear-based mind set to their children, who respond by cheating at school to get grades required for a top college, or taking steroids to bulk up for sports, or starving themselves to look thin enough for modeling. Or maybe they just give up and feel like losers. Whatever the result, this is distorted thinking, and it's poisoning a generation.

Fear of God's Wrath

Shouldn't we care about what God thinks of us? Shouldn't we desire his approval? Absolutely. In fact, the Bible refers to this as *fear*. "The fear of the Lord is the beginning of wisdom" (Proverbs 1:7).

Yet I find that religious fear can get distorted too. People may start out with a healthy desire to please the Lord, but they get swept into a rigid perfectionism driven by the terror of eternal damnation. They spend each day worrying that God will get them for committing one sin or another. In some cases, it's one major sin in the past that they still feel guilty for, or perhaps a general lifestyle from long ago that they deeply regret. Fear dominates their thinking so much that they can't truly accept forgiveness.

Fear may be the beginning of wisdom, but it's not the end. In fact, the New Testament tells us that "perfect love drives out fear" (1 John 4:18). Both testaments describe God as loving, eager to forgive us and welcome us back into a joyous relationship. One of the most glorious promises in Scripture is found earlier in John's first letter: "If we confess our sins, he is faithful and just and will forgive us our sins and purify us from all unrighteousness" (1 John 1:9).

God forgives *all* our sin—past, present, and future. We no longer need to carry the guilt, since Jesus paid for our sins on the cross. When we are unwilling to believe God's offer of complete forgiveness, we incarcerate ourselves in a prison cell of fear and doubt. We need to accept supernatural forgiveness—unconditional, undeserved, and limitless in scope.

Several years ago I counseled a college student who felt guilty about her sexual involvement with her boyfriend. She had confessed her sin to God, sought forgiveness from her boyfriend, and even shared the pain of her failure with her parents. Yet for several years afterward, she kept pleading with God for forgiveness. Because of her fear-induced doubt, she suffered many personal, spiritual, and interpersonal consequences. After many counseling sessions, she began to realize that God had truly forgiven her sins and actually "remembered them no more" (Jeremiah 31:34).

It is not humanly possible to forget many things in our past. God has given us minds that store memories for a long time. But the good news is we're also granted tremendous freedom to decide what to do with those memories. This young woman will think back on her past actions with regret and remorse, but she need not cling to those memories or use them to demean her own character. Instead, she can use them as a reminder of God's love. The Bible states, "As far as the east is from the west, so far has he removed our transgressions from us" (Psalm 103:12). That's a long way.

> It is not humanly possible to forget many things in our past. God has given us minds that store memories for a long time. But the good news is we're also granted tremendous freedom to decide what to do with those memories.

The choice is not between remembering your sin or forgetting it. It's already in your brain. The question is what you'll do with it. Will you let the memory of your sin cause you to doubt God and yourself, loading you down with unnecessary guilt and blocking your future relationship with God? Or will you let that memory help you to grow and change? Don't keep reminding God of your sins; he chooses not to remember them anymore. Let your memories of past failures trigger a spirit of praise and thanksgiving for God's gracious forgiveness.

47

Personal Evaluation.

1. I know that I am self-conscious and insecure in some areas of my life. Three of the most prominent areas of insecurity are:

   a. _____

   b. _____

   c. _____

2. Do you have an active "what if" diary in your mind and imagination? It might help to review the most worrisome at the end of each day and ask yourself what you can do and what you can expect God to do.

   _____

   _____

   _____

   _____

   _____

   _____

   _____

   _____

   _____

   _____

   _____

   _____

   _____

   _____

Practical Application

1. List current "fear knots" in your heart and separate them into your Circle of Control and Circle of Concern.

   Circle of Control

   _____

   _____

   _____

   _____

   Circle of Concern

   _____

   _____

   _____

   _____

2. Design a specific plan to deal with the issues that you listed in your Circle of Control.

   _____

   _____

   _____

   _____

   _____

   _____

3. Memorize Philippians 4:13—"I can do everything through him who gives me strength."

49

Prayerful Meditation

1. **Fear Not**—God will quiet my heart and meet my needs.

   "Do not be anxious about anything, but in every-thing by prayer and petition, with thanksgiving, present your requests to God" (Philippians 4:6).

2. **Fear Not**—God will protect me from being dominated by anxiety when feeling insecure personally and inadequate spiritually.

   "And the peace of God, which transcends all un-derstanding, will guard your heart and minds in Christ Jesus" (Philippians 4:7).

3. **Fear Not**—God will faithfully take up the slack when my needs go beyond my abilities.

   "And my God will meet all your needs according to his glorious riches in Christ Jesus" (Philip-pians 4:19).

Chapter Four
ALL TANGLED UP
How Fear Affects Our Emotions

"I think I must be going crazy," the woman told me.

While traveling in Germany, I spoke at a military chapel one Sunday morning and this woman came up at the end of the service, obviously very anxious. She said it was the first time she had been to church since her mother's sudden death a year-and-a-half earlier. Since that time her life had been an emotional roller coaster. In great detail she described the previous eighteen months, in which she had experienced anxiety attacks, fits of anger, excessive worry, and prevailing depression. Though she was on medication, she had made no attempt to get counseling. She was simply stewing in this collection of debilitating emotions. Then a friend had told her a psychologist would be speaking at the chapel service, and she decided to come and see if I could provide any help.

All the emotional symptoms she experienced were legitimate. In fact, when someone loses a loved one, it's rather common to go through new and confusing emotions. I assured her of this, but then I also suggested that her emotional "stew" might be stirred by fear—in her case a fear of death. We like to go through life pretending it will never end, but when someone close to us dies, we are shaken. Yes, there is sadness at the loss of this dear one, but there's also a grim reminder of our own mortality. That worries us, angers us, and depresses us. It takes a while for us to come to terms with this. Although the process is different for everybody, many people need a year or two.

Fear that wraps itself around our heart often triggers a chain reaction of other major emotions.

As I shared this with the woman in the chapel, she gained a new sense of hope. For the first time in months, she realized she was not "going crazy." And if she could sort through her fears, she felt she could bring some order to her chaotic feelings. Of course I also talked with her about renewing her relationship with God, so she would be spiritually ready for death whenever it would come.

I'm not denying that there are other root causes of emotional problems, but fear is often overlooked. If you are having trouble with feelings of anxiety, anger, or depression, it might help to ask yourself some important questions about any prevailing fear that has not been identified or dealt with. Could you find emotional health by unraveling your fear knots?

Emotional and mental illness in the U.S. has a frequency akin to cancer. Suicide is the third leading cause of death among teenagers. Anti-anxiety and anti-depression medication amounts to 230 million prescriptions each year. Stress-management seminars, DVDs, and books are multi-million dollar industries. People are desperately trying to cope with a wide range of emotional issues, but I believe many of these issues spring from a deep-rooted fear.

Fear that wraps itself around our heart often triggers a chain reaction of other major emotions. Anger, anxiety, depression, and worry are often symptoms of a heart tied up in fear knots. A man is angry because he fears losing power. A woman is anxious because she fears failure. Perhaps even now in your own life you are experiencing emotional struggles and have never considered that fear could be a major contributor. Let's briefly consider several fear-fueled emotions.

Anxiety

Anxiety seems to be the official emotion of our age, the basis of all neuroses, and the most pervasive psychological phenomenon of our time. It is as old as human existence, but the complexities and pace of modern life have alerted us to its presence and probably increased its influence. Anthropologists talk about the basic "fight or flight" instinct in humans. If some caveman was accosted by a saber-toothed tiger, he would find extra energy coursing through his system. That energy would help him fight the beast or flee. The problem with modern anxiety is that there's no saber-toothed tiger. We regularly feel that same instinct, but without any real cause. We live constantly with the fight-or-flight energy, but there's nothing to fight or flee. Oh, occasionally there's a real threat, but our anxiety keeps humming, even when the threat has passed.

You might think of it as a car engine racing at top speed, with the transmission in neutral. Lots of energy is expended, but for no purpose. Anxiety doesn't help us. It just overreacts to phantom issues. I love what Carol Kent said in her book *Taming Your Fears:* "Worry and anxiety give a small thing a big shadow." [NOTE 4]

53

Anxiety is, essentially, what I've been calling "manipulating fear." It's not the positive fear that empowers us to take control of a situation, to do something to meet the threat, to fight the tiger. No, it merely runs our engines, wasting our mental, physical, and spiritual energy.

Another way of understanding the pressure that chronic fear and anxiety cause comes from the field of engineering. In the field of engineering, the threshold for handling stress is defined by the limits of a material's ability to carry loads or withstand force. The same is true of us. We each have limitations. In engineering, a metal's response to stress is determined by its chemical makeup. For example, some steels will bend easily. Others, like alloy steels, will withstand higher pressures without bending. A metal coat hanger bends easily without breaking. A high alloy steel razor blade won't bend at all but will fracture when stressed to its limit. It is the same with the human ability to handle fear-inducing stressors in life. Our responses are, to some extent, determined by our individual characteristics; obviously, some people can take more than others. The woman I spoke with in Germany had a similar breaking point. Her mother's death awakened fears in her that she didn't know how to handle, and she lost her emotional balance.

> Times of physical relaxation and routine exercise have proven to be a great guard against anxiety.

Each of us has an emotional threshold limit, and we experience major difficulties when it is crossed. Fear can push us to that limit and beyond. Yet we can "steel" ourselves, so to speak, strengthening our emotions against the ravages of fear, with a few basic strategies.

Times of *physical relaxation* and *routine exercise* have proven to be a great guard against anxiety. Often our bodies store tension, making our minds and emotions more apt to feel anxiety. Maybe you've had times when you just felt jumpy, ill at ease, nervous, and for no good reason. In those cases it wouldn't take much to set you off. But if you take a break, maybe do some light exercise, breathe deeply, and meditate or pray, you might find your physical systems restoring to normal. As a psychologist and pastoral counselor for nearly forty years, I learned early how essential physical exercise is for me to maintain emotional balance. I walk five days a week and I can tell the difference in my emotional well-being when I miss several days in a row. Physical exercise is an absolute prerequisite to the quality of emotional health that will sustain you during fear-generating storms of life.

Mental focus is another important anti-anxiety strategy. Perhaps the "prayerful meditation" section at the end of each chapter will allow for focused evaluation of the fearful situation you are facing. Evaluate the situation you're feeling anxious about. What's really going on there? See what's in your Circle of Control and what's not. Get a realistic appraisal of what is, not what might be. See the "small thing" and not the "big shadow." This might involve a reordering of priorities.

Spiritual faith is another asset in anxious times. We'll discuss this more later, but for now I'll just give personal testimony to the value of prayer. I find wisdom in the Bible verse that says, "Be anxious for nothing, but in everything by prayer and supplication, with thanksgiving, let your requests be made known to God; and the peace of God which surpasses all understanding will guard your hearts and minds through Christ Jesus" (Philippians 4:6-7 NKJV). Imagine meditating on this. God promises us peace and protection in our minds and hearts…no "fear knots" necessary!

Anger

Who would think that angry attitudes and behavior could be linked to unmanaged fear? During a snowstorm in Bellevue, Washington, a man became so angry when his vehicle got stuck that he pulled a tire iron from the trunk and smashed all the windows. Then he hauled out a pistol and shot all four tires, reloaded, and emptied half of a second clip of bullets into the car. A police investigator on the scene called it a case of "autocide." The man was sober and rational but just very angry at his car, the police officer said. "He killed it."

Anger is a strange beast, and a dangerous one. We can laugh at the case of "autocide," because the man merely did damage to a machine, and one that he owned, but every day we hear about angry outbursts directed at other people, with devastating results. Item: A man attacks his neighbor because he fears that the neighbor's new driveway infringes on his property. Item: A woman slashes all the tires on her husband's car, parked in the "other woman's" driveway, because she fears losing her husband. Item: A political candidate maligns the character of his opponent because he fears the loss of power. The fear-filled personality adopts a corrupted golden rule: "Do to others before they can do to you." The people in these news stories were all, at least to some extent, manipulated by fear that triggered angry responses.

Not all anger is fear-related or fear-motivated. But when we have a chronic short fuse and a proneness to an angry spirit, often it is a result of a specific fear in our lives that we have not dealt with. It does not take long for fear to grow into full-blown rage.

While I was counseling a couple who were on the way to divorce court, it became apparent that the husband had an ugly and unruly anger problem. During one of the sessions, he began to verbally abuse his wife, despite my persistent objections. Finally I cried, "That's enough!" Shocked by my sudden vehemence, he stopped.

I asked their permission to conduct a rather unusual demonstration that could make a life-changing impact. "Let me show you how that feels," I said. So I began the theatrical and hopefully therapeutic drama. Placing a chair right in front of the husband, I stood on it, then leaned down, put my finger in his face and began to bellow, "How arrogant and unkind of you to verbally abuse your wife and totally disrupt this session. Now be quiet until I tell you it's your turn to talk. I will be the one who decides how this session will be conducted!"

I must say I rather enjoyed that moment of power. You can probably imagine the reaction of the shocked couple. Although I did not hear an "amen" from his wife, her nonverbal cues indicated that she did not want me to stop. As I stepped down from the chair, I noticed that the man's chin was quivering. Being a veteran counselor, I knew that the quivering-chin syndrome could be interpreted in one of two ways. Either my little demonstration had wonderfully connected with his heart and he was about to experience, for the first time in his life, a new insight into the destructive nature of anger, or he was so ticked off that he was going to explode—in my direction. Fortunately for me, the first option prevailed. He suddenly realized how his wife must have felt whenever he verbally attacked her. For the balance of the session, he was quiet, responsive, and compliant.

This strong, emotionally explosive husband was in many ways a little boy in a man's body. The thing that had triggered this angry outburst was fear. As we talked further, he confessed that he feared losing his job, losing his marriage, and losing control of an otherwise well-ordered life, but he couldn't own up to these feelings with his wife, daughter, or employer. Vulnerability and transparency were even more frightening to him. The only way he could react to the fear gripping his heart was to erupt in anger toward the one closest to him, his wife. There seemed to be a direct relationship between the intensity of his verbal abuse and his inner fears. "When I am pitching an angry fit," he explained, "I'm no longer aware of my feelings of fear and insecurity, I feel power and control."

Those comments are extremely insightful. For this husband—and for many, I suspect, with fear-based anger—the outburst is a distraction from the main problem. More than that, it's a quick-fix, a placebo. For the moment, his fear of powerlessness is salved by his angry display of power. But of course that doesn't last. And when the smoke clears, the anger has just made the situation worse.

The solutions to fear-caused anger are rather easy to identify, but difficult to put into practice. Vulnerability and

57

transparency are essential, allowing us to talk through our fears. This is especially challenging when a person feels ashamed to admit being afraid. (And this is particularly hard for men.) Beyond that, a protective measure might be the empathy exercise I tried with this husband. *How does it feel to be on the receiving end of an angry outburst?* That experience might shock a person into a new level of restraint.

People with chronic or dangerous anger issues should certainly seek professional counseling or look into anger management classes, video classes, or support groups. But my main point here is that your anger might be stoked by fear, and thus the best approach might involve untying your fear knots.

Depression

Fear throws our emotions out of balance, and the longer our deepest fears go unresolved, the greater the emotional cost. Immediate fears quickly bubble up in angry outbursts, and specific fears gather to create states of anxiety, but a long-lasting, general sense of fear can sap one's energy, driving a person into chronic depression.

Thousands of Americans are treated each year for depression and millions more suffer quietly without clinical treatment. "Depression is known as the 'common cold' of mental disorders and has been called 'the most widespread, serious, and costly psychiatric disease afflicting humankind today.'" [NOTE 5]

If anxiety is the revving of a car engine with the transmission in neutral, depression is the car running out of gas. It is a deadening of spirit. The senses stop sensing. The heart stops caring. It's hard to get up in the morning. It's hard to get out and do anything productive. In the grip of depression, people sleep too much or too little. They lose their appetite or give themselves up to all their appetites, succumbing to various addictive tendencies. They question the value of faith and relationships. In extreme cases, they contemplate suicide.

Fear isn't the only cause of depression, but I'm suggesting that it's a frequent cause, and often overlooked. When chronic fear keeps setting off the "fight or flight" alarm, it's only a matter of time before that alarm malfunctions. It's like the battery going dead in your smoke detector. You're so tired of gearing up to face your fears that you gear *down* on everything.

When chronic fear keeps setting off the "fight or flight" alarm, it's only a matter of time before that alarm malfunctions.

The last thing I want to do is to make anyone feel guilty about being depressed. That would just add to the problem. Nor do I want to suggest that there's an easy answer. You can't just decide to "put on a happy face" and dance out of the doldrums. Depression has afflicted people throughout all time—we even find it in the Bible. The prophet Elijah sank into a deep depression when he had to run for his life immediately after winning a great victory (1 Kings 19). Elsewhere, the Psalmist writes, "My thoughts trouble me and I am distraught. . . . My heart is in anguish within me; the terrors of death assail me. Fear and trembling have beset me; horror has overwhelmed me" (Psalms 55:2,4-5). In fact many of the writings in the Psalms and prophets reflect the depressed state of the author.

Yet I do want to suggest that we can begin the process of digging out from our fear-induced depression by examining those root fears. *What am I afraid of, and why?* Some might be afraid of getting hurt. Some might fear failure. Others might worry that they'll succeed and still be missing something. The range of possible fears is broad, and you'll never figure it out until you start talking it through or writing it down. A counselor—whether a psychologist, a pastor, or a wise friend—can help you do this.

A veteran counselor has the ability to discern between the client's symptoms and the sources of the problems presented. Many times emotional symptoms, like the ones we mentioned, are symptomatic of relentless fear knots of the heart. If we only address the symptoms and not the sources, inevitably it results in what I call "short-term gain, long-term pain." If the fear knots of your heart are not untied, they continue to disrupt emotional balance.

Personal Evaluation

1. Rate the following issues in order of how much they currently affect you.

___ Thinking irrationally (bouncing between behavior/ feelings/thoughts)

___ Experiencing unwanted angry outbursts

___ Extended times of despair and depression

___ A chronic uneasiness about life

___ Expecting the worst (especially in this situation:)

2. For your top-rated issue, answer this: How is fear involved? What are you afraid of?

_____

_____

_____

_____

_____

_____

_____

_____

_____

_____

3. What attempts have you made to deal with these problems?

   a. Professional counseling

_____

_____

_____

   b. Talking with friends or family

_____

_____

_____

   c. Self-control

_____

_____

_____

   d. Self-help books

_____

_____

_____

   e. Prayer

_____

_____

_____

   f. Other

_____

_____

_____

Practical Application

1. Memorize Philippians 4:6-7: "Do not be anxious about any-thing, but in everything, by prayer and petition, with thanks-giving, present your requests to God. And the peace of God, which transcends all understanding, will guard your hearts and minds in Christ Jesus." Replace "anything" with your particular problem and pray the verse every day.

2. Make a "worry list" and share it with your spouse or a close friend. Ask him or her to pray specifically every day for a week about one item on this list. You do the same. At the end of this week, talk with your confidant about the items each of you prayed about. Have those situations changed? Are you worrying less? Then try it again the next week with different issues.

_____

_____

_____

_____

_____

_____

_____

_____

_____

_____

_____

_____

Prayerful Meditation

1. **Fear Not**—God promises to be with me when I am facing fear.

    "Be strong and courageous. Do not be terrified; do not be discouraged, for the Lord your God will be with you wherever you go" (Joshua 1:9).

2. **Fear Not**—God promises peace as I concentrate on him.

    "You will keep him in perfect peace, whose mind is stayed on you, because he trusts in you" (Isaiah 26:3 NKJV).

3. **Fear Not**—God promises to protect me.

    "Do not be afraid. Stand still, and see the salvation of the Lord, which he will accomplish for you today. . . . The Lord will fight for you, and you shall hold your peace" (Exodus 14:13-14 NKJV).

Chapter Five
BODY DAMAGE
Physical Effects of Fear

John and Mary seemed to be a relatively stable couple. John was a very successful salesman, Mary was involved in the church, and their children were in college. One cold, wintry morning, while Mary was cleaning out John's suitcase after his return from a business trip, she discovered a receipt for a gift and motel reservation for two. Her world came crashing in around her.

Assuming that her husband had been with another woman on the trip, she was traumatized by the thought. This discovery unfurled deeply held fears. Not only was she fearing for the future of her marriage, she was also connecting with pain from the past. When Mary was a teenager, her father had been unfaithful to her mother, resulting in divorce. Since then, she'd been haunted by the fear that someday the same thing could happen to her. As long as her marriage was thriving, she could put those worries aside. But here she had evidence of infidelity, printed in black and white.

In similar situations, some might get very angry or very sad. Mary got very sick. Eventually, a form of paralysis set in and Mary temporarily lost the ability to walk. After consultation with a host of specialists, it became apparent that Mary's difficulty was rooted in her psychology—it was "psychophysiological," they said. Her emotional pain had been converted to a physical paralysis. How could she recover? As the experts explained it, her emotions were sending her a message through her body. She needed to figure out the meaning of that message.

It was clear that Mary and John had some work to do on their relationship. She also had to spend some time paying attention to her true feelings, rather than dismissing her fears and pretending she was feeling fine when she wasn't. According to the experts' scenario, it was that sort of blockade that forced her emotions to take drastic physical measures to get the message through. In time, with extensive counseling, she regained the full use of her legs. Also, she and her husband worked hard to renew their commitment.

That's an extreme case, to be sure, but it illustrates the major effects that unresolved fears can have on our bodies. We've already seen how fear can twist our thinking and distort our emotions. In this chapter we will see how unharnessed fear can actually damage our bodies.

I once taught a class on abnormal psychology, and one of the most intriguing sections in our curriculum had to do with the relationship between our mind, emotions, and body. Students are asked to digest such terms as: psychosomatic, somatoform, psychogenic, and psychophysiological. Each of these tongue twisters relates, in some fashion, to our body's response to our emotions. They indicate that the real pain we feel in some part of our body might not always have a physical trigger, but could in fact be caused by an uncontrolled emotion. In my counseling, I've found that the uncontrolled emotion is often fear.

Here's how it works. When we are faced with a threat, fear triggers the production of adrenaline and other stress hormones that prepare the body to fight or flee the impending danger. This defensive reaction increases the blood sugar, heart rate, blood pressure, and muscle tension, all of which provide the extra energy required for emergency actions. But if the sensation of fear persists once the emergency has passed, this extra energy remains. Our heart rate, blood pressure, and muscle tension continue on an elevated plane, and that which was intended for "emergency use only" begins to cause harm to the body. A pile of modern research confirms this: Constant tension raises the risk of illness.

Perhaps you have visited doctors over a span of years for various physical pains, and then your physician kindly suggested that you consider counseling. Maybe the suggestion offended you or hurt your feelings. Why can't doctors mind their own business? Well, that *is* their business. If they've ruled out various physical causes for your symptoms, they need to consider emotional causes as well.

Fear and Your Heart

I'll never forget one time when I was sitting in a crowded Atlanta airport. Because bad weather had delayed multiple flights, people packed the entire area, filling the chairs, sitting on the floor, and leaning against the walls. Even though the noise made it difficult to concentrate on the book I was reading, I finally managed to zone everything out.

Suddenly someone grabbed me from behind and yelled in my ear!

Talk about a heart rush! I let out a blood-curdling cry and just barely avoided propelling my book into the lap of the lady across from me, who also jumped and shrieked. In fact, everybody in the immediate area was momentarily startled.

I leaped to my feet and prepared to defend myself against whatever threat this was. To my surprise and great delight, there stood my pastor and friend, Dr. David Jeremiah! He had that "gotcha" look on his face. And just when I was about to launch into a scolding—"Where did you learn to behave this way?"—I realized that he was just returning the kind of prank I'd been playing on him for years. He'd probably learned this from me. So, while my heart kept racing, he stood there in the terminal laughing with great gusto. I wouldn't have thought that a man of the cloth could enjoy "payback time" so much!

An occasional temporary burst of heart-racing is normal and natural, equipping us to face potential danger, but it can become a problem when the fear-response becomes frequent or constant. In my case, after discovering that it was my friend who frightened me, I could relax. Even then, it took a few minutes to get my system back to its normal, "pre-fright" condition. What would have happened if another friend popped out of nowhere the next minute, and then another? That wasn't likely, but it's exactly the sort of thing that occurs when people magnify their own fears and focus on them. A heart that continually races will begin to weaken. Being on continual alert contributes not only to the possibility of an initial heart attack but increases the potential of a second one.

In the last generation or so, the awareness of this mind-body connection has changed the way doctors communicate with heart patients and others with serious illness. In the past, thinking that bad news might be alarming, doctors often tried to sugar-coat the situation. Some still do that today. But then they began to realize that people fear the worst, and in the absence of reliable information about their condition, they're likely to enter a damaging fear cycle, where every twinge creates new tension. But when cardiac arrest patients are informed about their disease, the dynamics of a heart attack, and the probabilities of further heart problems, they become less fearful.

The fear of the unknown is replaced by an understanding of what's happening. In my terms, they are able to sort out their situation between the Circle of Control and the Circle of Concern. They understand that there are certain things they can do to improve matters while there are still other factors beyond their control. In any case, research has shown that when well-informed, fewer cardiac patients suffer a second heart attack.

Fear and Cancer

A number of scientists have suggested that there is a "cancer-prone personality." This has aroused considerable controversy over the last few decades, but various studies have affirmed the basic idea—that certain emotional traits make people more vulnerable to cancer.

"First, a great tendency to hold resentment, and marked inability to forgive; (2) a tendency to self-pity; (3) a poor ability to develop and maintain meaningful long term relationships; and (4) a very poor self-image"--these were the traits identified by O. Carl Simonton and Stephanie Matthews-Simonton, early theorists on the subject. [NOTE 6]

"These qualities," the Simontons propose, "make it difficult for a person to deal with emotions at a constant level, to acknowledge negative feelings and then to deal with them." According to their theory, these "negative emotions" eventually express themselves in the body. Malignancy is thus despair that has been experienced biologically, despair at the level of the cell. [NOTE 7]

Although the emotion of fear is not specifically mentioned in these studies, I maintain that it exists in and around those emotions listed. Those prone to self-pity see themselves as victims of frightening forces. At the very least, this research demonstrates the connection between emotional turmoil and physical health. While proposed remedies range from creative to quacky, it has become increasingly clear that cancer treatment needs to focus on the whole person, body and soul.

69

Fear is often brought on by a cancer diagnosis; this research suggests that a pre-existing fearful personality might have made the patient vulnerable to begin with.

Fear and Your Immune System

Psychoneuroimmunology, or PNI, is a relatively new branch of psychology and medicine that studies the correlation between the nervous system and the immune systems. It has found that nerve endings work in cooperation with tissues that produce, develop, and store immune system cells. In addition, the immune system responds to chemical signals from the nervous system.[NOTE 8]

At UCLA, Dr. Margaret Kemeny found that the normal, fearful response to sudden danger can have a positive effect on the immune system, creating an increase in the immune responses. [NOTE 9] Does this disprove my point? Not at all. All along, I've been saying that fear is a healthy, natural response that can turn unhealthy and manipulative. A momentary stress-response to an immediate threat is an important survival tactic, and Kemeny says it helps future survival by strengthening the immune system.

But what happens when that momentary stress-response becomes prolonged? When the body is not allowed to resume its normal rhythms, but stays at a level of high-alert, the healthy effects are reversed. Numerous scientific studies have now suggested a strong link between high stress and low immunity. Fear, of course, is a major stress producer (and a stress aggravator). When fear becomes a long-term response—the situation I've been describing as "fear knots"--the immune system begins to break down, causing people to become more vulnerable to disease.

Fear and Pain Management

One of the purposes of natural childbirth training is learning how to respond to the fear-generating circumstance of

70

having a baby, and how to manage the physical response of pain. My wife and I took special classes in preparation for the birth of our second child to help "us" manage the natural emotion of fear and thereby reduce the intensity of physical pain. Breathing, concentration, coaching, and physical preparation were all part of the process. However, our journey together during the birthing process was not quite as smooth as it should have been.

At one point Marlene began to hyperventilate. Her fingers were stiff, a tingling sensation persisted in her feet and hands, and she began to panic. But she did not have to face the panic alone. Her fearless, and well-trained coach—that's me (ha!)—was prepared for such an emergency. They had taught us that in the event of hyperventilation, I should place a paper bag over her mouth and help her breathe into the bag. We had failed to notice, however, that the bag had a hole in it, and thus we were making the problem much worse. Even though I responded with precise confidence and followed my training procedures perfectly, Marlene's condition deteriorated. Now her whole body was stiff. I had managed to tie her fear knots even tighter. Being highly trained in psychology, I detected that her confidence level in her coach had taken a nosedive. Once I accepted the reality that our plan was not productive, I did what any composed coach would have done: I yelled "NURSE!" at the top of my lungs.

She brought a paper bag and soon Marlene's breathing returned to normal and baby daughter Kendra arrived on the scene.

Now don't miss the point of the story. Natural childbirth classes significantly diminish the power of fear and result in reducing the experience of pain. Marlene's ability to manage her response to a very frightening and painful situation made a difference.

Fear and Recovery From Illness

Not only can emotions contribute to physical illnesses, but the emotion of fear can significantly limit recovery from major physical problems. According to Dr. Thomas Delbanco of Harvard Medical School, "Uncertainty is the worst illness. The fear of the unknown can really be disabling. Even if the news is bad, people feel better if the uncertainty is dispelled." Based on this observation, he takes time to educate his patients about their illnesses and treatments. Fewer fears mean faster healing. [NOTE 10]

> "Uncertainty is the worst illness. The fear of the unknown can really be disabling."

Once, when my parents lived on a farm in Ohio, Dad began to have pains in his arm and chest and was having trouble breathing. Mom called 911. But it was a cold winter night, and a fierce arctic storm had covered the roads with ice, making travel nearly impossible. It took nearly two hours for the emergency team to get Dad to a hospital. When he arrived, he was in stable condition, so they transferred him to a hospital in Columbus where the doctors decided to do a new procedure using a rotoblater to clean out his arteries. He was awake during that procedure, and he heard the doctor say they had inadvertently cut an artery. The surgeon asked Dad's permission to do open-heart surgery if necessary.

Talk about fear! I can't imagine what Dad must have been feeling: to be lying there, helpless but conscious, in the hands of a surgical team, when a doctor basically says, "Oops!" Fortunately the medical staff responded with expert precision and were able to stop the bleeding without opening Dad up. The crisis was averted and he was on his way to recovery. His experience is now used in medical training classes and to help physicians know how to avert the problem or how to apply life-saving techniques in the event of a rotoblater mishap.

Now the challenge for Dad, and thousands like him, was to deal with post-event fears in a way that would provide him with the best opportunity for full recovery. For some, every physical symptom becomes an alarm that they are having another heart attack. Fear of future heart attacks actually contributes to the potential of a recurrence. Little by little Dad learned to deal with his fear-saturated experience with a growing confidence and faith that renews health and prevents relapse.

Psychiatrists at the Stanford University School of Medicine compared two sets of women with advanced cases of breast cancer. The members of one set joined a support group where they could share common fears and anxieties. The others did not participate in any support group. By this time the outcome should not surprise you. Those in the support group experienced less nausea from the treatments and were generally healthier and lived longer. The alleviation of long-term fear about their illness contributed significantly to their overall health and recovery.

Dr. Norman Cousins noticed this same bridge between positive emotions and the ability to fight cancer. He observed that the person who leaves the doctor's office in a state of fear and panic has a greater struggle ahead of him than the person whose fears have been calmed. Positive determination helps the body to produce its own "chemotherapy," he said, in the fight for better health, even in the fight against cancer. [NOTE 11]

We must be somewhat cautious in this whole area. I am not suggesting that we reject medical treatment in favor of just zoning out and thinking happy thoughts. This is not "mind over matter"— it's mind *and* matter working together. Medical treatment can do some amazing things, and I see this as a great gift from God. Yet there is an intricate and intimate relationship between the mind and the body, one that scientists are still beginning to understand. The fears that bother our souls can wreak havoc on our bodies, so it only makes sense to treat both the emotional and physical issues. As research has attested, a caring environment and the calming of fears can affect body chemistry in a positive way.

Fear and Laughter

It's hard to laugh when you're afraid. Oh, there's the occasional "nervous laugh," and some folks are known for their "gallows humor," but these are restricted, protected responses. A full-out, whole-body belly laugh is hard to achieve when your body is tense with fear. And yet that might be the best thing for you.

There is a proven relationship between our emotions, our bodies, and the positive impact of humor. When a person laughs heartily, blood pressure goes down, along with breathing rate and muscle tension. Laughter increases levels of endorphins, our natural painkilling, pleasure-giving hormones, and decreases levels of epinephrine, the stress hormone. It lowers blood sugar. Its benefits rival those of good exercise. One doctor calls it "inner jogging." Another prescribes, in addition to exercise, 15 minutes of laughter per day. [NOTE 12]

Norman Cousins, quoted earlier, pioneered research into the connection between laughter and good health. Diagnosed with heart disease and an extremely painful form of arthritis, he began watching Marx Brothers films in order to laugh more. "I made the joyous discovery that ten minutes of genuine belly laughter had an anesthetic effect and would give me at least two hours of pain-free sleep." [NOTE 13]

Elsewhere he commented on some of the laughter research that was still in its early stages. "Laughter may or may not activate the endorphins or enhance respiration, as some medical researchers contend. What seems clear, however, is that laughter is an antidote to apprehension and panic." [NOTE 14] This supports my point that fear and hearty laughter have trouble co-existing.

All of these thoughts echo a precept written thousands of years ago. In the book of Proverbs, wise King Solomon said, "A cheerful heart is good medicine, but a crushed spirit dries up the bones" (Proverbs 17:22). Three thousand years ago, the connection between human emotions and health was already postulated.

It's amazing it took modern science so long to catch up.

Personal Evaluation

1. Migraine headaches, backaches, sleeplessness can all be related to chronic fear. Do you suffer from any of these problems? Are there particular fears that might be contributing causes (for example, worry over financial stress)?

_____

_____

_____

_____

_____

_____

2. Think of the last time you were faced with fearful news or a frightening experience. How did you respond?

   a. Did you deal with it and continue on with your life?

   _____

   _____

   b. Did it continue to haunt you for days or weeks afterward?

   _____

   _____

   c. Are you still trying to overcome its control?

   _____

   _____

   If so, how could you rid yourself of the effects of this fear?

   _____

   _____

   _____

75

3. How often do you laugh? Is it possible that the absence of laughter could be slowing your ability to regain your health?

_____

_____

_____

_____

Practical Application

1. Not all physical problems are caused by emotional upheaval. However, the next time you have physical pain, take a few minutes to look back at the past couple of days to see if there are any possible emotional contributors. Write down those things that bother you emotionally which might be causing your body to react.

_____

_____

_____

_____

_____

_____

_____

_____

_____

_____

_____

_____

2. The Bible mentions nine positive qualities as "fruit" produced in a healthy life led by God's Spirit (Galatians 5:22-23):

love

joy

peace

patience

kindness

goodness

faithfulness

gentleness

self-control

Choose just one of these qualities and determine a specific way that you are going to begin developing it in your life today. Tomorrow, choose one more. At the end of each day try to recall how you displayed that particular spiritual trait. Before long you will have emptied the fruit basket and discovered a more fulfilling lifestyle.

3. Memorize Proverbs 3:7-8: "Do not be wise in your own eyes; fear the Lord and shun evil. This will bring health to your body and nourishment to your bones."

Prayerful Meditation

1. **Fear Not**—God has promised to give us rest from the battles of life.

> *"For I am the Lord, your God, who takes hold of your right hand and says to you, 'Do not fear; I will help you'" (Isaiah 41:13).*

77

2. **Fear Not**—God will give you needed strength and a song in your heart.

> *"Surely, God is my salvation, I will trust and not be afraid; the Lord, the Lord, is my strength and my song; he has become my salvation" (Isaiah 12:2).*

3. **Fear Not**—God is with you even in the most serious times.

> *"Even though I walk through the valley of the shadow of death, I will fear no evil; for you are with me; your rod and your staff, they comfort me" (Psalm 23:4).*

Chapter Six
FEAR KNOTS
DEVELOP YOUR FAITH
Learning to Count on God's Faithfulness

*Fires were burning out of con-*trol. I had to make a quick decision. Authorities in our San Diego community had told us to evacuate. Now I needed to figure out whether to stay and fight for my home or get to a safe place fast!

I made sure my wife and daughter moved to a safe place down the mountain, and then I gathered with neighbors to devise a house-saving plan. One friend provided fire hoses and a water truck. Others surrounded the house, manning regular garden hoses. Two men were on the roof of the house with fire hoses. When the fire jumped the highway below my home, we knew we had about ten minutes.

We got in a circle and prayed together. After hosing each other down and putting on masks to protect from the smoke, we waited for the firestorm to reach us. It was without doubt the most terrifying experience I had ever faced. The flames were 30-40 feet high on both sides of the house. The smoke was so thick we could barely see our hands in front of our faces. I was furiously hosing down the propane tank to keep it cool. I figured if I was going to die in this fire, I wanted to go quick! Twice I had to go to my knees because I could not breathe. The fire was sucking up all the available oxygen.

The firestorm moved by our home very quickly, with heat so intense that it melted an artificial plant on my back patio. After everybody else went home, I stayed in case there were spot fires. When I finally started driving down the mountain about 8 p.m., I discovered that the fire had moved down almost to the edge of the town. Fire was raging on both sides of the road, so I could not turn around. One car had been abandoned on the side of the road and was burning. I knew I was in deep trouble. Through the blinding smoke I could only manage to see the yellow line down the middle of the road, and I followed it. Finally I got out of the worst of the raging fire and drove on to safety.

Our home was saved, but sadly over three hundred homes within a few miles of our home were lost.

> There is an irrefutable relationship between fear and faith.

But there's more to this story. Following this terrible tragedy there was a firestorm of faith. Our church set up a command center and provided food, shelter, clothing and money to families who had lost everything. Out of the ashes of the fire, many individuals and families grew in their faith in God. One survivor, who later became involved in our church, stated, "I would never want to go through anything like this ever again. But thank God for the difference it has made in my life and the lives of all our family. We will never be the same. It was through the firestorm that we came to faith in Christ."

This sort of thing happens more often than you might think. Tragedy is often followed by a renewal of interest in spiritual matters. There is an irrefutable relationship between fear and faith. Fear in some ways is actually a prerequisite to spiritual growth.

This relationship is interactive as well. Fear leads to faith, and faith unravels fear. When we get a sense of who our God is, and when we understand that he cares about what happens to us, we can gain assurance in the most traumatic circumstances. Faith is the single most important contributor to untying fear knots.

Facing Dirt

During the war in Bosnia, Air Force Captain Scott O'Grady's fighter was hit by an SA-6 surface-to-air missile fired from a Bosnian-Serb stronghold. He was forced to eject from the flaming F-16. As he floated toward earth, he could see enemy soldiers below him, waiting for him to land. So, when he hit the ground, he took only seconds to get out of his parachute and hide.

For the next six days O'Grady experienced nearly constant terror as armed men searched for him, some coming within three to five feet as he lay motionless, covered with mud and leaves. "For the most part, my face was in the dirt," the airman says, "and I was just praying they wouldn't see me or hear me." One time a cow grazed on grass between his legs, with a herder nearby, and O'Grady managed to remain completely still, undetected.

After his dramatic rescue by U.S. marines, people wondered how he had gotten through this terrifying ordeal. "I prayed to God and asked Him for a lot of things, and He delivered throughout the entire time." When he prayed for rain, O'Grady said, God gave him rain. When he prayed, "Lord, let me at least have someone know I'm alive and maybe come rescue me," that night another pilot heard his radio call for help. Scott said he wasn't a hero--he was just a scared little bunny rabbit—but he trusted God's faithfulness throughout the time of terror. [NOTE 15]

"Do not fear, for I am with you," the Lord said through the prophet Isaiah. "Do not be dismayed, for I am your God. I will strengthen you and help you; I will uphold you" (Isaiah 41:10). This is not a random promise. As you flip through the Bible's pages, you'll find the words "fear not" and "don't be afraid" repeatedly. We see Bible characters in an assortment of terrifying situations, but God asks them to trust in him.

On the banks of the Red Sea, pursued by the Egyptian army, Moses brings God's message to the people: "Do not be afraid. Stand firm and you will see the deliverance the LORD will bring you today" (Exodus 14:13). Then the sea parted to provide an escape route.

A generation later, after Moses died, his gargantuan leadership task fell on Joshua. "Be strong and courageous," God told him. "Do not be terrified; do not be discouraged, for the LORD your God will be with you wherever you go" (Joshua 1:9).

Jeremiah was brutally honest as he described his calling as a prophet. Like the Air Force captain, he might have described himself as "a scared little bunny rabbit." In fact, he said, "I am only a child." But God had a task for him: "You must go to everyone I send you to and say whatever I command you. Do not be afraid of them, for I am with you and will rescue you" (Jeremiah 1:6-8).

Learning that his fiancée, Mary, was pregnant, Joseph wanted to separate himself from scandal and break off the engagement, but God said, "Do not be afraid to take Mary home as your wife, because what is conceived in her is from the Holy Spirit." One of the names of the newborn child would be Emmanuel, which means, "God with us."

Have you noticed a theme here? Fear is out of place, even in fearful situations, because *God is with us*. These people, and many others like them, were not asked to act out of courage or self-confidence or denial or determination or a positive mental outlook. They were invited to put their trust in the presence of God in the midst of heart-crunching fear knots. You see, it's not fear or faith. It's fear *and* faith. Jesus was over-whelmed with fear in the garden just hours before his cruel death on the cross. He had human fear and spiritual faith simultane-ously. And it is the same for us. We can never be godly enough, sincere enough or disciplined enough to be without fear. It is not an option for human beings to be without fear. But it's possible to overcome your human fears with spiritual faith.

Imagine a small boy, shopping with his father in a discount warehouse, who wanders away from his dad, staring in wonder at the tall shelves, big boxes, and bright lights. Suddenly a fork-lift backs across the aisle, beeping insistently. The wondrous surroundings immediately become frightening. The child looks around desperately. "Dad? Where's Dad?"

Just then, the big, familiar hand rests on his shoulder, and the little boy loses his fear. "Hi, Dad," he says, drawing a big breath. "I knew you were there all the time; I just couldn't see you at first."

Like this small boy, we may panic when we're suddenly thrust into frightening situations that temporarily distract us from our Heavenly Father's presence. But when we adopt a con-fidence in God's faithfulness, as a basic principle of our lives, we can quickly look up and say with great relief, "Hi, Lord. I knew you were there all the time."

We find then that the frightful situations become learning ex-periences. They're homework assignments in the course "Fear Knots & Fear Not's 101." Fear-drenched circumstances provide great opportunities for us to stretch our faith in God's faithful-ness. While facing fear/fear-not situations, those who trust God learn to lean on his promise to be with us in all things. We turn our eyes upward and feel God's strong hand on our shoulder. Fear magnifies our appreciation for our faithful God.

I know it's very difficult, while cowering beneath a bur-den of fear, to believe in God's faithfulness. But once we have dumped the fear-filled load, if we take time to look back at the experience, we will see how the tender shoots of our growing faith were protected and nurtured by the greenhouse of God's faithfulness. To put it another way, if we flex our feeble faith muscles as we enter the ring to spar with fear, then flex them again at the final bell, we will see tangible growth.

I will never forget the moment my friend and pastor, David Jeremiah, asked me to come to his office for a meeting. As I walked into the room, the atmosphere was quite sober, and I recognized immediately that his agenda was very serious. I sat down and heard David say, "Ken, I have some very disturbing news to share with you. I just returned from the doctor and he confirmed that I have cancer."

Cancer. The very word strikes fear into our hearts. It's a death sentence for many, a challenge for all. I was shocked by the news. I sat silently with my friend for a short time, tears coming to our eyes. Then we prayed together and began to develop a plan on sharing the news with his family, friends, and the others involved in our ministry.

Fear was a natural response to that situation, but it wasn't the ultimate response. I'd be lying if I told you we were fear-free in that first meeting or in the following weeks and months. The fear knots kept popping up in our hearts and among those around us, but we helped each other. We kept reminding each other—and ourselves—of God's faithfulness.

Pastor Jeremiah has been through two surgeries since then, and doctors have now declared that his cancer is in complete remission. As I've watched him through this crisis, I've seen how his relationship with God has been stretched. This life-threatening illness was met with a gradual growth of faith, hope, and love. Oh, checkup visits to the doctor have not been without fearful challenges, but by and large these years have been a journey from living in fear to living by faith.

I don't mean to imply that God will give every drama of your life a happy ending. He does not say, "Fear not, for

I will make everything go smoothly for you." While some people, like my friend David, are healed, others succumb to serious diseases. Some soldiers, like Scott O'Grady, receive miraculous protection, and others die in conflict. Sometimes the Lord will calm a storm, and other times he lets it rage. I can't explain this, and I don't know anyone who can. But I can tell you that the Lord remains faithful whatever the outcome.

Greg and Barbara Meeks were both involved in church work—Greg as an ordained minister and Barbara as a director of youth and children's ministries. They had both believed in God's healing power for many years. They had even taught about it. When their daughter, twelve-year-old Christen, was diagnosed with cancer, they just knew that God would heal her. Their church and many friends and neighbors prayed regularly for Christen's healing, believing that God would come through. They claimed Bible promises. As their daughter went through months of chemotherapy and other treatment, and those months became years, Greg and Barbara kept assuring each other of God's healing power.

But two weeks before her fifteenth birthday, Christen died.

As you can imagine, the faith of this family was tested to the limit. How could God take this sweet girl away from them? They didn't have answers, but they trusted that God was still with them, and that God was with Christen, even after she drew her last breath. At her funeral, many of her high school friends heard her parents talk about the ultimate healing that Christen now knew, because she was in heaven where she could no longer be touched by pain and illness. Those in attendance saw a faith that had been stretched by sorrow. This family's faith in God's faithfulness during this very difficult time had a profound impact on both youth and adults in their small community.

Many are eager to give testimony of how God wonderfully provided for them when they had a great need, or delivered them from a fiery furnace. As God reminded Jeremiah, "I am the Lord, the God of all mankind. Is anything too hard for me?" (Jeremiah 32:27). Nothing is too hard for God. We joyfully point to his salvation, praise him for answered prayer, and proclaim his faithfulness. And well we should. But the greatest test of trust is how we respond when lions tear us limb from limb, when the final chapter of adversity does not have a storybook ending.

I think of the faith of those three courageous Jews in Bible times who stepped into the fiery furnace—Shadrach, Meshach, and Abednego. They had refused to bow down before the king's idol, and they were willing to pay the price—being tossed into a furnace of blazing fire. As they were sent to their punishment, the king taunted them: "What god will be able to rescue you from my hand?"

Here's how they responded: "We do not need to defend ourselves before you in this matter. If we are thrown into the blazing furnace, the God we serve is able to save us from it, and he will rescue us from your hand, O king. *But even if he does not*, we want you to know, O king, that we will not serve your gods or worship the image of gold you have set up" (Daniel 3:15-18).

> Christians are not exempt from the reality of terminal disease, the ravages of drought, earthquakes, and floods, the effects of budget cuts and joblessness, and threats of religious or political persecution.

Even while radio and TV evangelists boom the errant gospel of health, wealth, and prosperity, we must listen carefully for the faith-filled response of these three young heroes. God can work miracles, but will he? That's up to him. If we trust in God's faithfulness to sustain us, develop us, calm us, use us, and eventually bring us home to heaven, we also need to trust his faithfulness when frightful circumstances do not bring a happy ending. Christians are not exempt from the reality of terminal disease, the ravages of drought, earthquakes, and floods, the effects of budget cuts and joblessness, and threats of religious or political persecution.

The eleventh chapter of the New Testament book of Hebrews is often known as "the faith chapter." It chronicles the exploits of those followers of God whose faith led them to do great things—Abraham, Moses, David, and so on. It refers to many who, through faith, escaped harm and some who were even raised from the dead. But it also tells about others who "were tortured and refused to be released, so that they might gain a better resurrection. Some faced jeers and flogging, while still others were chained and put in prison. They were stoned; they were sawed in two; they were put to death by the sword. They went about in sheepskins and goatskins, destitute, persecuted and mistreated . . . they wandered in deserts and mountains and in caves and holes in the ground" (verses 35-38). Through it all, they persisted in trusting the faithfulness of God. With the strength of God's adequacy they battled the inborn fear knots that attended their suffering.

We need to cultivate daily reminders of the absolute faithfulness of God. In good times and bad, in success and failure, God is faithful. When we focus on his faithfulness on our behalf, we will begin the process of untying the fear knots around our heart.

"Do not be afraid," God says, "for I am with you." He promises his presence. Whatever situations are striking terror in your heart these days, he says he will stand with you. Whatever the outcome, you can count on his company.

Oh, remember those three young men stepping into the furnace? As the king sat down to watch their suffering, he called to his advisers, "Weren't there three men that we tied up and threw into the fire? . . . Look! I see four men walking around in the fire, unbound and unharmed, and the fourth looks like a son of the gods."

Again and again, he steps into the fire with us. Count on it.

Personal Evaluation

1. What recent event in your life provided an opportunity to be stretched in your faith?

    _____

    _____

    _____

2. Now that you have time to evaluate, how could you have responded differently?

    _____

    _____

    _____

    _____

    _____

3. What did God bring into your life that allowed you to deal with the fear knots?

    _____

    _____

    _____

    _____

    _____

Practical Application

1. Start a fear knots journal and then keep track of the faith-building scripture, words of encouragement from others and heart-felt prayers that sustain you at just the right moments.

2. Initiate a "fear knots" prayer team. Meet occasionally with a select few trusted friends and develop a meaningful transparency. Share the issues of life that are currently cultivating fear in your heart. Encourage one another and pray for one another. It will change your life forever.

3. Listen to inspiring, faith-generating music when you have opportunity. Memorize scripture that directly lines up with the fear knots of life and the fear not's of God's Word.

Prayerful Meditation

1. **Fear Not**—God gives peace and hope.

   "May the God of hope fill you with all joy and peace as you trust in him, so that you may overflow with hope by the power of the Holy Spirit" (Romans 15:13).

2. **Fear Not**—God is our help in trouble.

   "God is our refuge and strength, an ever-present help in trouble. Therefore we will not fear . . ." (Psalms 46:1).

3. **Fear Not**—God is faithful.

   "Because of the LORD's great love we are not consumed, for his compassions never fail. They are new every morning; great is your faithfulness" (Lamentations 3:22-23).

Chapter Seven
THE FAITH AND FEAR CONNECTION
What It Means to Trust in God's Faithfulness

Some years ago, I traveled with my family to New York City for a few days of sightseeing. Our youngest daughter Kara was visiting the big city for the first time, so Marlene and I tried to show her as much as we could. It was all a bit intimidating--the rush, the crowds, and the noise. We used the subway to get around town, and that was also a strange atmosphere, especially for the inexperienced Kara. The many unkempt individuals lounging around kept us careful and alert. I kept my daughter close beside me, but it was my wife who found herself in a situation that both created fear and exercised her faith.

Rushing to get uptown, we purchased our subway tokens, and Kara and I quickly pushed through the turnstile and jumped on the train—only to look back to see that Marlene was still behind the turnstile. Her token had gotten stuck and she couldn't get through. I'll never forget the look on her face as she watched us disappear down the tracks.

This was before the time of cell phones, mind you. My wife is a devout believer, but believe me, the response I saw in her countenance at that moment was fear, not faith. She stepped back into the waiting area, lonely and scared. Separated from her family in a strange city, she might encounter all sorts of dangers. How would she find us again?

Fortunately, I had just asked the man in the token booth which stop to take for Central Park and Broadway. Remembering that conversation, Marlene decided she would just wait for the next train and hope to find us at that stop. Still, the fears flew through her heart as she waited, clutching her purse tightly. Would some ne'er-do-well prey upon a woman standing alone on the platform, obviously unfamiliar with the territory?

In her purse Marlene always carries a miniature Bible that has one verse from every book in the Bible. For solace, she started reading that to pass the time, beginning with the Genesis verse. Halfway through the Old Testament, she found the verse from Esther especially comforting. In the selected verse, the young queen was taking a huge risk, pleading with the king to save her people, and she said, "I go in unto the king. . . and if I perish, I perish." The faith of Esther fully acknowledged the danger of her situation, but also understood that she had a higher calling. Whatever would happen or wouldn't happen on that subway platform in the next few minutes, Marlene knew she was in God's good hands.

The train came and she boarded, getting off at the stop near Central Park and Broadway. There she found Kara and me, waiting anxiously for her.

I appreciate what Max Lucado wrote in his book *The Eye of the Storm*: "Biographies of bold disciples begin with chapters of honest terror. Fear of death. Fear of failure. Fear of loneliness. Fear of a wasted life. Faith begins when you see God on the mountain and you are in the valley and you know that you're too weak to make the climb. You see what you need . . . you see what you have . . . and it isn't enough . . . but He is . . . *Faith that begins with fear will end up nearer the Father.* [NOTE 16]

There is an intimate connection between faith and fear. The most faith-driven people are not fearless. They experience fear like anyone else, but they transform it into faith. Like Marlene on the subway platform, they recognize the danger of the moment, but they also realize that's not the whole story. Faith does not deny reality; it perceives the full reality of a situation—not only the danger or difficulty, but also the power and promise of God.

In the last chapter we discussed God's absolute faithfulness. What is the appropriate response to his faithfulness? Faith, of course, but that's not all. The New Testament gives us a valuable triad of responses: faith, hope, and love. Chances are, you've attended a wedding where the Love Chapter was read—1 Corinthians 13. Previewing that chapter, the apostle wrote, "I will show you the most excellent way" (1 Corinthians 12:31), and he concluded that chapter saying, "And now these three remain: faith, hope and love, but the greatest of these is love" (13:13).

Love is, of course, his main theme, and he saves that for last, but let's not overlook the two other qualities listed. In this chapter and the next two, we'll talk about these three aspects of growing spirituality and how they can all combine to transform our fears into something far more positive. Faith, hope and love are the spiritual hands that untie the fear knots of our hearts.

First, **faith**. What does it look like? How do we practice it? How does it interact with our daily fears?

The story is told from a previous century about the great daredevil Blondin, who walked a tightrope stretched across Niagara Falls. He once asked his audience if they believed he could walk across with a person on his back. Already dazzled by his amazing ability, most of them nodded agreement. Then he asked for volunteers.

It's one thing to believe *that* something is true. It's quite another to trust in someone, and to rest your life on their ability. Perhaps you were nodding in agreement as you read the previous chapter on God's faithfulness. But believing that he is faithful is only half the battle. We need to trust in his faithfulness, and that trust needs to govern our attitude and actions in the most trying circumstances.

Right after high school I joined the Army Paratroopers. I had the privilege of qualifying as Senior Jumper (over thirty jumps) and then as a Jumpmaster (the guy who invites the troopers to leave the plane at just the right time). The training was very challenging and the boldly stated goal of the drill sergeant was to cause you to quit. And nearly a third of each class does just that. So what makes the difference between success and failure?

Faith.

I've observed this again and again. One of the key qualities of a good paratrooper is faith. Faith that the many hours of training will pay off. Faith that the Jumpmaster knows the wind and the drop zone. Faith that the parachute will open up. Faith that other troopers will fulfill their duty to insure safety for all. But here's another interesting factor: In spite of all the mental drilling, convincing ourselves that we were invincible, there was never a jump that was devoid of fear. Yes, we practiced faith—we had to—but it was always the necessary combination of faith and fear that got us through. There is no such thing as facing fearful circumstances without fear. Faith does not eradicate fear; it gives the measure of confidence necessary to face the fears.

> Faith does not eradicate fear; it gives the measure of confidence necessary to face the fears.

Faith Provokes Trials

"In this world you will have trouble," Jesus told his disciples (John 16:33).

One of those disciples, Peter, later wrote, "Dear friends, do not be surprised at the painful trial you are suffering, as though something strange were happening to you" (1 Peter 4:12).

Frightful situations will occur. That's a fact of life. More than that, it's a fact of *faith*. The Bible keeps telling us that people of faith will be magnets for tough circumstances. Peter goes on to explain that Christians have the privilege to "participate in the sufferings of Christ."

When the New Testament talks about the suffering of Christians, it's often referring to specific violence or slander or prejudice that first-century believers were experiencing. Such persecution has recurred in various places and times since then, but not so much in our culture. Still, it should be no surprise if we experience some opposition to our faith. People may treat us badly because we're Christians.

But there are other troubles we may face as well. The apostle Paul said that we join in a general "frustration" that the whole creation experiences, "groaning inwardly" as we wait for God's ultimate redemption (Romans 8:18-23). Life is hard, and frightening circumstances may overwhelm us.

We also get a hint in Scripture that our faith opens us up to a refining process that can often be unpleasant. The story of Job begins with a strange encounter, in which God brags to the devil about the faith of Job. Of course the devil then asks permission to torment Job, taking his wealth, his health, and his family. Would he remain faithful when things got tough? The point is that Job's great faith *provoked* his trials. Peter assures his readers: ". . . now for a little while you may have had to suffer grief in all kinds of trials. These have come so that your faith—of greater worth than gold, which perishes even though refined by fire—may be proved genuine and may result in praise, glory and honor when Jesus Christ is revealed" (1 Peter 1:6-7).

If you're going through difficult times, don't think that God is giving up on you. Some people compound their fears by worrying that they have alienated God in some way and he's getting back at them by making their lives so hard. But Scripture teaches otherwise. Our trials are often an indication that we are living by faith, and God just wants to make us stronger. The best response is not fear, but (believe it or not) joy. "We also rejoice in our sufferings," Paul writes, "because we know that suffering produces perseverance; perseverance, character; and character, hope" (Romans 5:3-4).

Faith Perseveres Under Trials

So our faith can bring about difficulties, but it also gets us through them. "Consider it pure joy, my brothers, whenever you face trials of many kinds," writes James, "because you know that the testing of your faith develops perseverance. Perseverance must finish its work so that you may be mature and complete, not lacking anything" (James 1:2-4).

This passage uses a fascinating word, translated here "of many kinds." In the original Greek, the word has the sense of "multicolored." Our difficulties will come in many different shades, as if we were at the paint store looking through those color strips. But Peter uses the same word to describe God's grace "in its various forms" (1 Peter 4:10). God has a grace for any trial we face. Whatever the particular hue of our difficulty, God will match it. We can trust in his support, and that trust keeps us going.

Athletes often use the phrase "no pain, no gain" as they're suffering through their hundredth drill, their fiftieth crunch, their twentieth rep. It hurts, but it's worth it, because they recognize the strength or skill that will result. In the same way, faith is built up by exercise. We learn to trust God in our most daunting situations, and that trust drives us forward. You might feel some spiritual pain as you're forced to exercise your faith in fear-filled trials. Great faith is always born out of great challenges, and the Lord promises that these challenges will develop our perseverance. Perseverance is when your hands and feet keep on working even though your head says they can't do it.

Every fall the monarch caterpillar crawls to the end of a twig, fashions a meticulously fabricated cocoon around itself, slams the door and goes to sleep for the winter. The following spring something utterly miraculous happens—out comes a beautiful monarch butterfly. If we were to walk past the cocoon just as the butterfly emerges from its magic chamber, we would see a fierce struggle going on. The emerging insect pushes, pulls, and wiggles its way out, sometimes falling back in complete exhaustion. Perhaps we would be tempted to help, maybe taking some tweezers and pull back the opening ever so slightly in order to free the butterfly from its potential coffin.

> Perseverance is when your hands and feet keep on working even though your head says they can't do it.

Well-meaning though such a gesture would be, it would seal the butterfly's doom. For the very struggle to break from the cocoon strengthens its wings, making them strong enough to fly. If the butterfly does not struggle to get out, it will be condemned to crawl among the twigs. Unable to fly, it will starve to death or become dinner for a neighboring bird. Prerequisites for transforming the ugly little caterpillar into a beautiful butterfly are time in the cocoon and the energy-demanding trial of struggling to get out.

Much like the monarch butterfly, our ultimate beauty and final form are directly influenced by the fear-filled experiences we struggle within our lives. So when we face a major challenge will we be paralyzed by fear or stretched in faith? Every promise of God should keep us standing firm, filled with faith, not cowering in fear.

Faith Provides Courage During Trials

It was recorded as the shortest commencement speech in history. This special speaker, who had been pursued for years by the Ivy League schools, finally accepted an invitation extended by his former grade school, Harrow. The irony is that, as a student at Harrow, he had been in the lower third of his class and showed little potential. Still he had graduated, gone on to a university, and made a name for himself. Now he was invited back to speak to the young graduates. After all the preliminaries, he moved slowly to the lectern, paused, cleared his throat and spoke these words: "Young gentlemen, never give in! Never give in! Never, never, never. Never—in anything great or small, large or petty— never give in except to convictions of honor and good sense." He then returned to the comfortable chair on the platform and sat down. The crowd, at first stunned into silence, spontaneously leaped to their feet and delivered a standing ovation that lasted for many minutes! They understood what Sir Winston Churchill was communicating to the graduates.

At a time in which the world faced some of the most fearful circumstances in history, Churchill issued messages of hope, faith, and determination. His words of inspiration struck a greater blow to the enemy in World War II than any navy destroyer could have. His fears were legitimate, but his persevering faith was contagious.

It seems that the greater the challenge, the greater the opportunity for genuine growth. Extracting all the spiritual value from a trial is like grabbing an orange half, thrusting it down upon the juicer, then pressing and turning for all you're worth. The intense effort extracts every drop of juice from the orange. Then, once you pick out all the seeds, you have the satisfaction of pouring that tasty nectar into a glass and drinking it down. In a sense, the more intense your efforts, the more fruitful and refreshing the results.

There is a direct relationship between the intensity of the trial and the potential for increased faith. Before deciding on taking the climb, many of the 300,000 people who ascend Mount Fuji each year stop to consider the challenge of a nine-to-sixteen-mile climb (add another three to five miles for slippage on loose ash). With some apprehension, they read about the route up the mountain (paying close attention to rest stops). Then they begin to prepare their bodies for the strain before they ever fly to Japan. They walk during their lunch hours, and on weekends climb mountains near their homes. But the price they have to pay for the experience seems small when they anticipate the sunrise greeting them in reward for their all-night climb. They look forward to recording the picturesque event on their cameras and proudly donning their "I climbed Mount Fuji" T-shirts.

> There is a direct relationship between the price paid and delight in a job well done, especially when the challenge is fear-filled, requiring courage and faith—coping with fear, paying the price, and finishing the course.

When the big day arrives they stand at the foot of Fuji, trying to see the top in the dark. Then, step by step, they begin the steep climb, feeling their way, slipping on volcanic ash. As they conquer the last summit, the dreamed-of sunrise and deep sense of achievement finally become reality—as well as the T-shirt. They return home standing a little taller, holding their heads a little higher, stepping a little lighter because their confidence has grown. After all, they climbed Fuji! Having the faith-driven courage/faith to conquer fearful challenges sweetens the reward when the task is completed.

There is a direct relationship between the price paid and delight in a job well done, especially when the challenge is fear-filled, requiring courage and faith—coping with fear, paying the price, and finishing the course. Fear tempts us to quit when the going gets tough, but faith supplies the courage to endure hardships and trials.

Consecrated Fear

We've been talking about two types of fear, manipulating and motivating, but there's a third we need to consider. I call it "consecrated fear." The Bible often talks about "the fear of the Lord," but always in a positive way. It's called "a fountain of life" (Proverbs 14:27) and "the beginning of wisdom" (Psalms 111:10). The fear of the Lord, we're told, brings delight and blessing, protecting us and lengthening our lives.

This is obviously not a paralyzing fear; it's energizing. Other kinds of fear can tear relationships apart, but this fear is the foundation of a growing relationship with God. It has to do with loyalty, love, respect, reverence, and submission to his amazing love. Cultivating a greater love for God marginalizes the power of human fear.

How do we develop such a consecrated fear? I'd like you to consider five ways, with a little wordplay to help you remember.

Acknowledge his position. This consecrated fear begins with a sense that God is God and you are not. He is the creator and sustainer of the universe. He has power far beyond your own, and while this power is fearsome, his love is just as strong. He cares what we do, and he wants what's best for us.

The psalmist says, "As a father has compassion on his children, so the LORD has compassion on those who fear him" (Psalms 103:13). That father-image is very helpful (and, of course, we find it often in the New Testament). In a good home, a little child has a healthy fear of parents—wanting to please them, depending on their provision—within a context of love.

100

Ask for his protection. There's an enjoyable adventure story in the Old Testament that vividly depicts God's protective power. An enemy king suspected that his battle plans were being supernaturally revealed to the prophet Elisha, who was relaying them to the Israelite king. So a military unit was dispatched to capture the prophet. Elisha's faithful servant looked out one morning and saw enemy soldiers surrounding the town. You can imagine the fear knot that caused. "What shall we do?" he cried.

"Don't be afraid," Elisha responded. "Those who are with us are more than those who are with them." Then he prayed that God would "open the eyes" of his servant, which God did. Then the servant looked again and saw "the hills full of horses and chariots of fire all around Elisha" (2 Kings 6:8-17).

> When we are tied up in fear knots, we see only part of the picture. As we move into "consecrated fear," we can see the threats that surround us, but we also see that our protection is far greater.

God's army had been there all the time. All the servant needed was a faith-filled, heavenly perspective. When we are tied up in fear knots, we see only part of the picture. As we move into "consecrated fear," we can see the threats that surround us, but we also see that our protection is far greater.

Accept his presence. In Elisha's case, the enemy army was miraculously struck blind and the threat was neutralized. But there are other stories, in Scripture and from more recent history, where believers have suffered pain and even death. God does not promise physical survival in every dangerous situation. He does promise to be with us. I think of Stephen, the church's first martyr, who was brutally stoned to death, but at the end received a vision of Jesus in heaven (Acts 7). "Fear not, for I am with you," is God's continual reassurance (Isaiah 41:10).

With consecrated fear, we recognize that we don't know the physical outcome of our situation, but we know the Lord stands beside us for eternity.

Apply his plan. Do you have one of those GPS trackers in your car? These gadgets bounce signals off satellites to determine where you are and then figure out the best way to get where you're going. In spite of all this high-tech wizardry, there are still drivers who insist on trying to find their own way. They ignore the GPS directions and strike out on another route, often with disappointing results.

Some people do the same thing with God's instructions. They ignore his plan for their lives and go their own way, often with disappointing results. When we live our lives in the consecrated fear of God, we understand that he knows better than we do. He is our Maker, our Guide, our Friend. We trust that he wants what's best for us, and he certainly *knows* what's best for us. It only makes sense to live the way he wants.

Access his power. The prophet Elijah saw the awesome power of God up close and personal. He challenged hundreds of false prophets to a bake-off, you might say. His opponents spent all day trying to call fire from heaven to consume a sacrifice they had prepared. It didn't happen. But when it was Elijah's turn, he prayed, and God sent fire. In his consecrated reverence for Almighty God, Elijah accessed divine power and won a great victory.

> Faith means counting on God's power in good times and bad, whether we're savoring victory or nursing our wounds.

But the next chapter tells a very different story. Embarrassed by the spectacle, wicked Queen Jezebel announced her plans to kill Elijah, and so the prophet went on the run. Consecrated fear turned to cowardly fear as he high-tailed it to the desert. There he languished in depression and even suicidal thoughts until he was reminded that God was still in charge.

Faith means counting on God's power in good times and bad, whether we're savoring victory or nursing our wounds. The amazing strength of the awesome God is within his people, just waiting to be tapped.

Personal Evaluation

1. As you think about the fearful situations that have troubled you over the past six months, would you say your perspective was more of fear or faith, or somewhere in between? How would it change things if your perspective moved more toward faith?

_____

_____

_____

_____

_____

_____

_____

_____

_____

_____

_____

_____

_____

_____

_____

2. What is one way I might . . .

. . . acknowledge God's position?

_____

_____

_____

. . . ask for his protection?

_____

_____

_____

. . . accept his presence?

_____

_____

_____

. . . apply his plan?

_____

_____

_____

. . . access his power?

_____

_____

_____

3 What one person has taught you the most about a persevering faith? What qualities have you seen in this person?

_____

_____

_____

_____

_____

Practical Application

1 Make a point every day to pray the following prayer so that God can help you adjust your perspective. "Lord Jesus, open my eyes to better see your power, protection, presence, and plan. Thank you for your promises."

2 Write down one thing that is troubling you right now. Now see how you can adjust your perspective of the problem by seeing it through the eyes of God's power, protection, presence, or plan.

_____

_____

_____

_____

_____

3 Memorize Jeremiah 33:3: "Call me and I will answer you and show you great and unsearchable things you do not know."

Prayerful Meditation

1. **Fear Not**—We have freedom to see the fear-inducing challenges of life from a heavenly perspective.

   "Therefore we will not fear, though the earth give away and the mountains fall into the heart of the sea, though its waters roar and foam, and the mountains quake with their surging" (Psalm 46:2).

2. **Fear Not**—I will trust God and not fear what others can do to me.

   "In God, whose word I praise, in God I trust; I will not be afraid. What can mortal man do to me?" (Psalm 56:4).

3. **Fear Not**—God's Word provides confidence and will help us rest and sleep.

   "When you lie down, you will not be afraid; when you lie down, your sleep will be sweet. . . . Have no fear of sudden disaster or of the ruin that overtakes the wicked, for the Lord will be your confidence and will keep your foot from being snared" (Proverbs 3:24-26).

Chapter Eight
HOPE
Faith in the Future Tense

Lori sought my counseling as she entered college. Not a good student in high school, she was admitted on academic probation. As we talked, it became obvious that she fully expected to be a poor college student as well. She didn't want to fail, but she was so intimidated by her fear of failure that she literally had no energy to meet the academic expectations of her new school. Her fears were based on a sense of hopelessness. She had no hope of a good outcome, and so she was defeated before she even started.

We talked at length about her situation. I urged her to let the past go, to work hard in the present, and to trust God with the future. More than anything, I wanted to instill in her a sense of hope. The future *could* turn out well. She *could* succeed. It was possible, if she worked at it. Slowly she began to gain a more positive vision of the future. Her transformation was stunning. Soon she was studying with confidence and enjoying academic success. Lori had gone from intimidation to inspiration.

Hopeless is probably the bleakest word in our language. Without hope, fear invades the soul and leaves it in despair; we give up and become victims. Sometimes social scientists talk about "learned helplessness" among those who have stopped trying to fend for themselves. On a spiritual plane, we could talk about "learned hopelessness." After a series of hope-crushing circumstances, people can start believing that, no matter what they do, no matter how diligent their efforts, no matter how determined they are, it just won't make any difference. They have been disappointed time and time again, and there's no longer any place for hope in their hearts.

> *Hopeless* is probably the bleakest word in our language. Without hope, fear invades the soul and leaves it in despair; we give up and become victims.

This is a woeful condition. As one proverb succinctly states, "Hope deferred makes the heart sick" (Proverbs 13:12).

But we're looking at the "most excellent way" of living described in the New Testament—faith, hope, and love. These qualities can empower us, taming and transforming our fears. So what is this "hope," and how can it change us?

The Future Tense

Hope is faith in the future tense. We could define faith as a firm conviction in God that affects our responses to difficult situations. Hope is similar, but it leans forward. Hope fills us with confident expectation for a better tomorrow, and so the present challenge is merely a bump in the road. Hope shows us that road, giving us a sense of getting somewhere. With that mind set, hope gives us the confidence we need to hang in there until we triumph over negative circumstances. Hope spurs the athlete to train and increase his strength. Hope inspires the musician to perfect her performance. Hope enables us to face that surgery, invest that money, take those classes, because we believe the present risk and sacrifice are worth the outcome. Hope is never merely a self-generated pep rally that invigorates and excites us; rather, it is a hardy confidence to look beyond the here and now and glimpse a promising future. Martin Luther said that everything that is done in the world is done by hope.

When I possess this "confident expectation," I have the courage to do what I must in terrifying circumstances. This confidence is not based on my own ability, but on my faith in God's power to create a blessed future.

Consider the black-belt karate expert who can break a brick with his bare hand. He must approach that task with utter confidence, his mind completely focused on its successful completion. Or what about the football team that faces a better-ranked foe? Whatever the rankings, the team must believe that winning is possible. That will keep them playing their best until the final whistle. Without a sense of hope, the game is lost before the kickoff.

Recently sportswriters scoffed when a coach whose football team had just eked into the playoffs declared that they should be the "favorites" to win the Super Bowl. Was this foolish overconfidence? No, it was hope, a solid expectation that inspired his team, which then shocked everyone by reeling off two playoff wins against supposedly stronger opponents.

A sick person with hope has a better chance of a rapid recovery than the person without hope. According to Norman Cousins, "The patient's hopes are the physician's secret weapon. They are the hidden ingredients in any prescription." This phenomenon is attested by many others. Hope seems to energize our physical systems so that healing can occur—and sometimes it even happens when the experts consider the disease an unbeatable foe. When a patient with a terminal disease says, "I'm going to beat it," is it just a case of wishful thinking? No! It's a mobilizing of the patient's physical, emotional, and mental forces to move forward in this struggle. The immediate task for an ailing person is to *get better*, and the hopeful person meets that task with confident expectation. If the situation seems utterly hopeless, why bother?

But let's consider again what the hopeful person is confident *about*. The athlete expects a victory and the patient a recovery, but hope involves far more than that. When our hope is based on faith *in God*, our hope is in him too. There's a helpful saying some Christians use: "We don't know what the future holds, but we know who holds the future." That answers our question. The athlete might lose the game and, more seriously, the patient might succumb to the illness. Even with hope, the outcome isn't always the way we script it. Still, we have a confident expectation that God will be with us in the process, that we will find strength and comfort, and that he is accomplishing his ultimate purpose.

> Hope-filled people are not defeated in times of hardship—not necessarily because they expect things to get better, but because they can see God's purpose even in their pain.

Hope-filled people are not defeated in times of hardship—not necessarily because they expect things to get better, but because they can see God's purpose even in their pain. Things may not always work out exactly as we envision, or as we want, but our ultimate purpose—experiencing and sharing God's love—will be fulfilled by the power of God's Spirit within us.

Remember Yesterday's Victories

When you are going through a fear-filled experience and feel that your hope is as weak and shaky as a newborn foal, remember that your hope is not in your own power, but in God's—and he has plenty. This is one of the most frequent themes in the Bible: *Remember*! Several of the psalms focus on the mighty acts of God, how he "brought his people out [of Egypt] like a flock," leading "them like sheep through the desert," guiding them "safely, so they were unafraid" (Psalm 78:52-53). The psalmist reminds us to "tell the next generation the praiseworthy deeds of the Lord, his power, and the wonders he has done" (Psalm 78:4).

Much of biblical history involves the people of God forgetting about his power, and then being reminded again. The nation that was miraculously brought out of Egypt balked at venturing into Canaan. They forgot how God had insulated them from the plagues in Egypt, drowned their enemies in the Red Sea, led them through the desert with a cloud by day and a pillar of fire by night, and quenched their thirst in the arid desert by causing water to gush out of rocks. Yet, "They willfully put God to the test by demanding the food they craved. They spoke against God, saying, 'Can God spread a table in the desert? When he struck the rock, water gushed out, and streams flowed abundantly. But can he also give us food? Can he supply meat for his people?'" (Psalm 78:18-20). And God did just that. He caused manna to drop from the sky so that the people had more than enough to eat.

Such faithful care should have provoked the people to trust in God with a courageous faith and confident hope. It should have challenged them to manage any future fears and anxious moments with a spontaneous and abundant hope. But it didn't. "They forgot what he had done, the wonders he had shown them" (v. 11). When they forgot what God had already done, fear rushed in to fill the vacancy left by faith's glaring absence, which in turn gave way to complaint and a nasty spirit of discontent. Their fear-blinded memory led to their fear-fueled murmuring. Fear has the power to close our minds to all God has done for us.

God repeatedly told the Israelites, and continues to tell us, of his faithfulness. He knows we are prone to forget him. Once we disregard his unchanging promise to care for us today and tomorrow with the same fidelity he has shown in the past, unbelief and all its ugly children—including fear—tighten the ropes around our hearts.

Ironically, it's often when we bask in the blessings God has given us in the past that our memories grow dim. Perhaps God has given you a great job, and now you're worried that you'll lose it. Perhaps he has enabled you to live in a lovely home, and now you're fretting over the payments. Remember the source of those blessings and trust him to care for you in the future. As they wandered in the wilderness, God warned his people about this very tendency: "When the LORD your God brings you into . . . a land with large, flourishing cities you did not build, houses filled with all kinds of good things you did not provide, wells you did not dig, and vineyards and olive groves you did not plant—then when you eat and are satisfied, be careful that you do not forget the LORD, who brought you out of Egypt, out of the land of slavery" (Deuteronomy 6:10-12).

> Hope remembers. It reviews God's past deeds of love and power, and it expects more of the same in the future. A good memory of God's blessing and protection in the past is another essential element in untying fear knots in our heart.

And I have to laugh a little at the way Jesus chided his disciples when they were worried about getting enough food. "Don't you remember? When I broke the five loaves for the five thousand, how many basketfuls of pieces did you pick up?" (Mark 8:18-19). They had seen him feed a crowd with a fish sandwich! Why couldn't they trust him to provide what they needed? I laugh, but I also realize that we all do that sort of thing. Forgetting God's power in the past, we fear for the future, and hope is diminished.

Hope remembers. It reviews God's past deeds of love and power, and it expects more of the same in the future. A good memory of God's blessing and protection in the past is another essential element in untying fear knots in our heart.

Tap Into God's Power

When the gigantic warrior was talking trash about the Lord Almighty, the shepherd boy David stepped up to oppose him. "Am I a dog that you come at me with sticks?" bellowed Goliath. It's not clear whether he was referring to the slingshot David held or the fact that David himself looked like a twig compared to the tree-like giant. The disparity in their size didn't bother the boy. He came before Goliath with hope in the Lord, confident of the task before him. God had helped him in his shepherding, in run-ins with a bear and a lion; surely God would help him defeat a blaspheming giant.

"You come against me with sword and spear and javelin," David announced, "but I come against you in the name of the LORD Almighty, the God of the armies of Israel, whom you have defied. This day the LORD will hand you over to me, and I'll strike you down . . . All those gathered here will know that it is not by sword or spear that the LORD saves; for the battle is the LORD'S, and he will give all of you into our hands" (1 Samuel 17:45-47).

You probably know how this turned out. The boy beat the behemoth by slinging a well-aimed stone.

When God assigns a fear-filled task to us, we can claim the same hope that David experienced. We can echo the words of Paul, "I can do everything through him who gives me strength" (Philippians 4:13). This is nothing to boast about. It's not our power at work here, but God's. It's like plugging in a lamp. The lamp shines by tapping into a much larger power supply.

I think back to the experience of Jesus' disciples during the week of his crucifixion. They had entered Jerusalem to the sounds of cheering, but there must have been fear deep within them. Their leader was headed toward a violent death. He had warned them of this.

As they ate their last supper with Jesus, there was thick tension in the air. And as the trial and crucifixion unfolded, they scattered, fearing for their own lives. Traumatized by the loss of their Lord, filled with uncertainty, how could they reconcile the promise of his presence, peace, comfort, courage, wisdom, and joy, with his devastating death? And beyond the spiritual questions, they faced the basic question of survival. Would the soldiers come for them next? Would they be tried as traitors too? The disciples gathered in secret, fearing for their lives.

Then came the hope-saturated news! He's ALIVE!

A flurry of activity. Women intending to offer the body a proper burial were met by an angel, who said, "Do not be afraid, for I know that you are looking for Jesus, who was crucified. He is not here; he has risen, just as he said" (Matthew 28:5-6). Peter and John raced to the tomb to find it empty. Mary Magdalene reported meeting with Jesus in the garden near the tomb. Other women saw him too. His first words to them were, "Do not be afraid" (Matthew 28:10). Two travelers had seen him on the road. Then he appeared to the disciples as they cowered in the upper room. "Peace be with you," he said—a common greeting, but now it held special meaning. Peace. Their world had turned topsy-turvy, but now their master promised peace. The Prince of Peace was assuring them that he held power even over death.

All of God's promises were now validated, forever insured by the resurrection power of Jesus Christ. Forty days later at the feast of Pentecost, those once-timid disciples received the power of the Holy Spirit and preached openly in Jerusalem. No more were they plagued with fear of what would happen to them. No longer would they be overcome by feelings of doubt and dread. They became people who "turned the world upside down" (Acts 17:6).

"Do not be afraid." "Peace be with you." The resurrected Jesus comes to us again and again offering his vast resources. Since Jesus has power over death, we can be assured that he also has power over any threatening circumstances in our lives. This hope is an "anchor for the soul, firm and secure" (Hebrews 6:19). When we feel that our lifeboat is about to go under, he secures us. As we claim this hope, we build a storehouse of strength that enables us to endure the fears of this life.

Find Encouragement in Hope

Several years ago, I was flying to a seminar in Chicago. I customarily leave my Bible out on the plane's tray table as I review my seminar notes. On this trip a middle-aged couple sat next to me. The lady, noticing the Bible, nudged me and asked, "Are you a pastor, priest, clergyman or what?" Then she added, "Do you have any prayers for the ill?" When I asked what she meant, she explained that her husband, seated by the window, was dying of cancer. In fact, their trip was a farewell to their family; then he would return home to die.

When she asked me to pray for her husband, I asked if they believed in the Bible. They replied that they did. For the next half hour I shared many verses from God's Word about death, suffering, hope, and eternity. After she and her husband took a rest-room break, they asked if I would occupy the middle seat and tell them both more about God. It was not long before both of them asked Jesus Christ into their hearts.

A couple of weeks later, I talked to the man on the phone. He admitted that he was somewhat afraid to die, but not with the dread that once gripped him. Now both he and his wife understood the reality of pain and loss in death and separation, but the impact was clearly softened by the glorious truth of eternal hope. He died a few days later, never to know fear again.

Hope gives us an assurance that goes beyond this earthly life. When the members of the Thessalonian church worried about what happened to believers who died, the apostle Paul offered strong comfort, "so that you may not grieve as others do who have no hope" (1 Thessalonians 4:13 NRSV). For many in our world, physical death is the complete and utter end, but we have the hope of eternity with the Lord. We need not fear death, because we know he is waiting for us.

The man I met on the plane knew he was dying, but his new-found faith gave him hope. It was not the confident expectation that his cancer would vanish. Miracles do happen, but this was not the hope he was looking for. He needed to know what was beyond the grave. There was still the pain of loss, for both this man and his wife, and there was some fear, but the Holy Spirit now lived within him, to whisper comfort and peace.

Don't Quit!

The concert hall was packed, and it was just a few minutes before the great pianist Ignacy Paderewski was to take the stage. As the story goes, a small boy slipped away from his parents' care and crept up to the stage. Sitting down at the huge grand piano, he began to play "Chopsticks." Red-faced ushers ran up the aisles toward the stage, intent upon unseating the child. Before they got there, however, Paderewski quickly put on his tuxedo jacket, walked on stage, and stood behind the boy. With his arms outstretched on either side of the child, he began to improvise an accompaniment to "Chopsticks." All the time, he was whispering to the boy, "Don't quit! Don't quit! Don't quit!" The crowd broke out in a spontaneous applause.

Many times, when we are faced with fear-inducing circumstances that rob us of hope, we are tempted to quit. But

116

the Holy Spirit of God puts his loving arms around us and keeps whispering in our heart this hope-generating encouragement, "Don't quit! Don't quit! Don't quit!"

Personal Evaluation

1. Is there a particular area of your life where the future looks rather bleak to you? How would a greater hope in God change that outlook?

_____

_____

_____

_____

_____

_____

_____

2. Can you think of a time in the past when you needed God's strength and he was there for you? What happened? How did you know it was God helping you?

_____

_____

_____

_____

_____

_____

_____

3. Is there a person you know who would be characterized as "full of hope"? How does that person affect others (including you)? What is one thing you could do to become more like that person?

_____

_____

_____

_____

_____

_____

_____

_____

Practical Application

1. Memorize Jeremiah 29:11—"For I know the plans I have for you,' declares the LORD, 'plans to prosper you and not to harm you, plans to give you hope and a future."

2. Hope is looking to the future with confidence, even though its content is unknown. List what you consider the three most important future issues or situations in which you need spiritual hope or confident expectation. For each of these, jot down what you think is the "worst case" and "best case" of how things will turn out. But leave another column for "God's power." How could God work in this situation to make something good happen—even if it's not in either your worst-case or best-case scenarios? You'll want to pray about this before filling in that column.

118

a. Situation:

_____

_____

Worst Case:

_____

_____

Best Case:

_____

_____

God's Power:

_____

_____

b Situation:

_____

_____

Worst Case:

_____

_____

Best Case:

_____

_____

God's Power:

_____

_____

c Situation:

_____

_____

Worst Case:

_____

_____

Best Case:

_____

_____

God's Power:

_____

_____

3. *Hope* is a great biblical word, with slightly different nuances in different scripture references. So do your own study of the term. Start with these verses:

Ruth 1:12

1 Chronicles 29:15

Job 13:15

Psalms 25:3

Psalms 33:18

Psalms 42:5,11

Psalms 130:5

Proverbs 23:18

Isaiah 40:31

Jeremiah 29:11

Lamentations 3:17-25

Zechariah 9:12

Romans 4:18

Romans 8:18-25

Romans 15:4,13

Colossians 1:27

1 Thessalonians 4:13

1 Timothy 6:17

Hebrews 6:19

Hebrews 11:1

1 Peter 3:15

1 John 3:3

Prayerful Meditation

1. **Fear Not**—Hope is the endurance we have because of God's truth.

   "Blessed is he whose help is the God of Jacob, whose hope is in the LORD his God" (Psalms 146:5).

2. **Fear Not**—God encourages us through hope.

   "May our Lord Jesus Christ himself and God our Father, who loved us and by his grace gave us eternal encouragement and good hope, encourage your hearts and strengthen you in every good deed and word" (2 Thessalonians 2:16-17).

3. **Fear Not**—Our joy and peace are not spoiled by fear-causing circumstances.

   "May the God of hope fill you with all joy and peace as you trust in him, so that you may overflow with hope by the power of the Holy Spirit" (Romans 15:13).

121

Chapter Nine
COMMUNICATE LOVE
Perfect Love Drives Away Fear

My son Mark was in the second grade and had always enjoyed school. So it surprised us when he began to resist getting ready in the morning. It became a battle for us to get him to school each day. Obviously there was some sort of emotional struggle going on within him—it was even affecting his sleep.

We finally caught on that he was afraid of his teacher.

So we decided to check this teacher out for ourselves. Meeting with Mr. Kolb, we discovered that he was a bit on the non-traditional side in how he dressed and his demeanor was a little angry, edgy and impatient. Maybe this was what bothered Mark. In any case, we decided to pray for Mr. Kolb each night as a family. As a family we also bought him a Christmas present, a book about Jesus.

We saw a dramatic transformation in Mark's attitude as he began seeking ways to show God's love to Mr. Kolb. Literally and dramatically, Mark's fear disappeared, and his Christian love for the teacher became a motivation to go to school.

Right after Christmas vacation, Mr. Kolb asked to meet with Marlene and me. He wanted us to be the first to know that, as a result of Mark's love, our prayers, and the book, he had accepted Christ as Savior over the school break. Over the years since, he has stayed in touch with Mark and even attended his high school graduation, again expressing his thanksgiving for a little boy's love.

"Perfect love drives out fear," the Bible says (1 John 4:18). In context, that verse is talking about our love for the Lord and our fear of his judgment, but I believe there's a general principle that applies to all our relationships with God and with other people. Chronic fear crowds love out of our hearts. When we're concerned only about ourselves, we can easily cultivate a fretful, cowardly lifestyle, unwilling to risk what we have. But love is all about reaching out, taking chances, courageously seeking the benefit of others.

By the way, when John wrote about perfect love driving out fear, he used a muscular verb. It means to throw or hurl, to get rid of—as we do with our garbage, or stones in the path of the lawn mower. Perfect love violently thrusts fear out of our lives.

God Loved Us First

"We love because he first loved us," John writes (1 John 4:19). God is the source of love. He puts the love in our hearts, and he leads us to share that love with others. We show love in his way, toward the people he wants to love. Is there someone you have a hard time loving because they don't deserve it? That shouldn't stop you, because God's love isn't based on what people deserve. If it were, we'd all be in big trouble. "God demonstrates his own love for us in this: While we were still sinners, Christ died for us" (Romans 5:8). If God loves the un-lovely, shouldn't we?

Thus, John says, "Everyone who loves has been born of God and knows God. Whoever does not love does not know God, because God is love" (4:7-8). So, we reason, since we have been born of God and know God and love God, it should be easy to love others and therefore be free of fear. Sounds easy--but we all know it's not. Fear is also at the root of our unwillingness to love. We are afraid that our needs or wants won't be met, so we build walls instead of bridges in relationships with those who have the potential to deprive us of what we want. "What causes fights and quarrels among you?" writes James in his analysis of human conflict. "Don't they come from your desires that battle within you? You want something but don't get it. You kill and covet, but you cannot have what you want. You quarrel and fight" (James 4:1-2). So it appears that a lack of love springs from fear, but it also leads to fear. Without God's help it becomes a hopeless cycle.

God's love breaks us out of that downward spiral. The New Testament illustrates all those fears and desires and quarrels being crucified with Christ and buried. "We died to sin; how can we live in it any longer?"(Romans 6:2). The love-gift of Jesus' sacrificial death sets us free to live in love. "Therefore do not let sin reign in your mortal body so that you obey its evil desires . . . .For sin shall not be your master"(Romans 6:14). We trade in our life of self-obsessed fear for a life motivated by love. "For Christ's love *compels* us," the apostle Paul explains, using another muscular verb. ". . . He died for all, that those who live should no longer live for themselves but for him who died for them and was raised again" (2 Corinthians 5:14-15).

So God's love is not only an inspiration to us, or something to bolster our courage—his loving actions have *empowered* us to move from fear to love. The old ways are gone; everything is new. Fear is part of the old regime. As part of God's new creation, we live in love.

When we begin to grasp the implications of God's amazing love, we realize that we don't have to be afraid of anyone or anything.

- We will not fear going hungry or thirsty because our loving Heavenly Father, who feeds birds and clothes flowers, is even more concerned with providing for us (Matthew 6:25-26).

- We will not fear evildoers or even the devil because "the Lord is the stronghold of my life—of whom shall I be afraid? When evil men advance against me . . . they will stumble and fall" (Psalm 27:1-2).

- We will not fear terrorists or attacks from foreign nations. "You may say to yourselves, 'These nations are stronger than we are' . . . But do not be afraid of them" (Deuteronomy 7:17-18). The psalmist adds, "I will not fear the tens of thousands drawn up against me on every side" (Psalm 3:6).

- We will not fear physical harm because we trust that God will either protect us or equip us to deal with any injury.

The promises of Scripture are wide-ranging. We can safely hide under the cover of God's protective wings (Psalm 91:4); his loving presence never leaves us (Matthew 28:20); Psalm 103 says he redeems our lives from destruction and "satisfies my desires with good things" (v. 4-5). "The Lord is with me," sings another psalmist, "I will not be afraid. What can man do to me?" (Psalm 118:6).

Calling us "more than conquerors," the apostle Paul declares, "I am convinced that neither death nor life, neither angels nor demons, neither the present nor the future, nor any powers, neither height nor depth, nor anything else in all creation, will be able to separate us from the love of God that is in Christ

Jesus our Lord" (Romans 8:37-39). Rejoicing in this truth frees us to love those whom we might otherwise have reason to fear.

God is not just the source of love; he is love (1 John 4:15). To know God is to embrace ultimate love. Because this truth is so all-encompassing, it is the first truth taught to little children in Sunday school. We may take it for granted, like the air we breathe. But this foundational truth is worthy of celebration. Let's rejoice in God's love.

God Will Always Love You

God's love is not limited by time or turmoil. Often we question things that happen in our lives or in the lives of others that seem harsh and unloving. We ask God, as Job did, "Why have you made me your target? Have I become a burden to you?" Or, "If I have sinned, what have I done to you, O watcher of men?" (Job 7:17,20).

We do go through times of trouble, but that doesn't mean God has stopped loving us. In the context of his boundless love, the Lord tends to the details of our daily lives, even keeping track of the number of hairs on our heads, but he never loses sight of his greater purpose, building us, shaping us, for his glory. Sometimes that requires rigorous training or unpleasant discipline. We are his beloved children, and "the Lord disciplines those he loves" (Hebrews 12:6). The book of Hebrews explains that God lets us go through some painful, even fearful times out of love, as a form of discipline, so that we can be made stronger. "Later on . . . it produces a harvest of righteousness and peace for those who have been trained by it" (Hebrews 12:11).

Sometimes God uses other people in this process, whether they know it or not. For example, when Joseph's brothers sold him as a slave, they did not realize that they were part of a master plan which eventually benefited Joseph, his entire family, and the whole nation of Israel. But Joseph rejoiced in the truth of God's sovereign care and could later say to his brothers, "Do not be distressed and do not be angry with yourselves for selling me here, because it was to save lives that God sent me ahead of you" (Genesis 45:5). Later, he chided his brothers, "You intended to harm me, but God intended it for good to accomplish what is now being done, the saving of many lives" (Genesis 50:20). Rejoicing in this truth freed Joseph to love his brothers.

We need not be afraid when trials come our way. These are indications that the Lord loves us. He cares enough for us to keep working on us, chipping away the rough edges, crafting us into vessels of delight.

God's Most Excellent Way

The thirteenth chapter of Paul's first epistle to the Corinthians is a stunning description of love. After using poetic comparisons to establish the importance of love, the apostle gets down to definitions. What does love look like? How do we actually live in this "most excellent way"?

"Love is patient, love is kind. It does not envy, it does not boast, it is not proud. It is not rude, it is not self-seeking, it is not easily angered, it keeps no record of wrongs. Love does not delight in evil but rejoices with the truth. It always protects, always trusts, always hopes, always perseveres. Love never fails." (1 Corinthians 13:4-8).

Let's take a closer look at these descriptions.

"Love is patient." In other words, we have to work at it. Love-motivated patience develops slowly, one victory after another, until we know how to love ultimately.

"Love is kind." When we love, we don't try to wound others with harmful deeds or destructive speech. Elsewhere Paul wrote, "Do not let any unwholesome talk come out of your mouths, but only what is helpful for building others up

according to their needs. . . . Be kind and compassionate to one another" (Ephesians 5:29,32). By contrast, unkindness is often fear-motivated or fear-related, trying to get ahead by tearing others down. Even if others are rude, you can make the loving choice to be kind. You can guard your tongue, grit your teeth, measure your words, and be kind and compassionate.

"It does not envy, it does not boast, it is not proud. It is not rude, it is not self-seeking, it is not easily angered, it keeps no record of wrongs." Being aware of the fact that you are pretty good at loving might cause you to puff up with pride, and again love would be lost.

"Love does not delight in evil but rejoices with the truth." The "truth" we rejoice in is God's truth, which the Holy Spirit breathes through our lives. Then the miracle of love begins— without our trying to force its growth. One by one, our fears are engulfed by love. The miracle begins with finding joy, peace, and power in the Word of God.

Perfect love "always protects, always trusts, always hopes, always perseveres. Love never fails." When we see others as fellow heirs of the grace of God, love flourishes and fear wilts. Perfect love drives out fear.

We cannot learn "the most excellent way" in one day. But we begin by embracing the Love that God sent to us—the Lord Jesus Christ. Then we start to live as Christ lived. Little by little we will embrace love's ingredients until we know how perfect love can toss fear out of our lives.

You can imagine the culture shock that greeted Eric and Janet Jeffery, a couple in their seventies, when they first entered a high school classroom as volunteer tutors. They were clearly out of their element, and shivering with apprehension. But they were concerned about teenagers, and this love conquered their fears. They decided to roll up their sleeves and help out.

They started by tutoring two students. Their loving dedication made a difference, and soon others came to them for help. They begin to enlist other senior citizens to join them, and the number of students being tutored grew to fifty and beyond.

Soon, as a direct result of their stepping out to demonstrate the love of Christ to at-risk high school students, every public school in Escondido, California, was requesting tutors from the Jefferys' group. What's more, the relationships established have benefited the students in other ways as well. The Jeffery's report that more than seventy-five students have elected to attend a Christian summer camp, and twenty-five have come to know the Lord. What a powerful love! And to think, this unique ministry could easily have been short-circuited by fear. Instead, it was driven forward by love.

Faith conquers fear, hope gives the endurance necessary to withstand fear, and love tosses out the remnants of any fear that is left.

God bestows three divine treasures, we're told at the end of that great "love chapter"—faith, hope, love. "But the greatest of these is love" (1 Corinthians 13:13). Faith conquers fear, hope gives the endurance necessary to withstand fear, and love tosses out the remnants of any fear that is left. All three are essential to untie the fear knots of our hearts, and all three are built into our lives by the same means—knowing, believing, and applying the Word of God.

Finish Strong

You probably don't know the name of Derek Redmond. A gifted runner, he held the British record in the 400-meter at age 19, and there were high hopes for his performance in the Olympics. But in the 1988 games he was scratched from the race just ten minutes before it started, because of an injury to his Achilles tendon. That meant four more years of healing and training and hoping.

Derek's father, Jim, went with him to the 1992 games in Barcelona. Jim had always supported his son's athletic efforts, and was usually in the stands for major races. He had talked with his son about past disappointments and future hopes. No matter what, he said, you need to finish this race.

The qualifying round began, and Derek jumped out to an early lead. Sixty-five thousand fans cheered him on, including his father. Suddenly, on the backstretch, Derek heard a pop. From his seat high in the stands, Jim Redmond saw his son clutch his right leg in pain, take a few hops, and fall down on the track. He had pulled his hamstring. A stretcher was brought out, but Derek refused it. "I am going to finish this race!" he exclaimed. Getting back on his feet, he half-hopped, half-hobbled toward the finish line. The other runners had passed him. The race had been won, but it wasn't over. The crowd was stunned and moved by the sight of this injured racer struggling on.

Meanwhile, Jim had jumped out of his seat and rushed down toward the track. He had no credentials to be there, but he jumped over a railing and evaded security guards, saying, "Get out of my way! That's my son out there and I'm going to help him!"

Finally the father reached the son and hugged him. "I'm here, son," he said. "We'll finish together."

The crowd continued to roar as the two moved down the track, Derek leaning on his dad's strong arms. A few steps from the finish line, Jim let go and allowed his son to cross on his own strength.

It was one of the greatest moments in Olympic history. [NOTE 17]

Have you been hobbled by fear? As you go through the race of life, have you stumbled and fallen? Are you afraid that failure will be your constant companion? Well, you have a heavenly Father who's willing to pick you up and walk with you. "I'm here, my child," he whispers. "We'll finish together." And step by step you can lean on his loving arms.

131

Personal Evaluation

1. We find a number of characteristics of love in 1 Corinthians 13. Which of these do you see strongly in your life, and which need improvement?

Characteristic	Strong	OK	Needs Improvement
Patient			
Kind			
Not Envious			
Not Boastful			
Not Proud			
Not Rude			
Not Self-Seeking			
Not Easily Angered			
Keeps No Record of Wrongs			
Does Not Delight in Evil			
Protects			
Trusts			
Hopes			
Perseveres			

2. In the last three days, in what specific ways have I experienced God's love? (Or three weeks?)

_____

_____

_____

_____

_____

3. In the last three days, in what specific ways have I shown God's love to others? (Or three weeks?)

_____

_____

_____

_____

Practical Application

1. Memorize 1 John 4:18a—"There is no fear in love. But perfect love drives out fear."

2. What one person in your circle of influence best illustrates biblical love? List three specific characteristics of this person that can be found in 1 Corinthians 13 (or in the list under "Personal Evaluation" on the previous page).

   a. _____

   b. _____

   c. _____

3. Can you identify three people you know who seem to be living in fear? What is one loving thing you could do for each of them that would help to reduce their fears? Be specific. Then, do these loving actions.

_____

_____

_____

_____

_____

_____

_____

_____

_____

_____

Prayerful Meditation

1. **Fear Not**—Having received God's love, we can share it with others.

   > *"For God did not give us a spirit of timidity, but a spirit of power, of love and of self-discipline"* *(1 Timothy 1:7).*

2. **Fear Not**—God's love keeps me safe in his holy arms.

   > *"The LORD is my light and my salvation— whom shall I fear? The LORD is the stronghold of my life— of whom shall I be afraid?"* *(Psalms 27:1).*

3. **Fear Not**—God's love is personal and he holds us in his protective care.

> *"Indeed, the very hairs of your head are all numbered. Don't be afraid; you are worth more than many sparrows" (Luke 12:7).*

Notes

1. Associated Press 2:54 p.m. ET, 11/12/07, dateline Albany, NY. Wansink's research was to be published in The Leadership Quarterly.

2. Douglas Pasternak, Neil Boyce, and Terence Samuel, "Tools of Mass Destruction," *U.S. News and World Report*, Oct. 29, 2001, p. 14.

3. Ibid.

4. Carol Kent, Tame Your Fears and Transform Them into Faith, Confidence and Action (Colorado Springs: NavPress Group, 1993), p. 55.

5. Gary Collins, *Christian Counseling, A Comprehensive Guide* (Dallas: Word Publishing, 1988), p. 78.

6. Maggie Scarf, *Psychology Today*, Sept. 1980, p. 37.

7. Ibid.

8. Dana H. Bovbjerg, "Psychoneuroimmunology: Implications for Oncology?" *Cancer*, Feb. 1, 1991, pp. 828ff.

9. Margaret Kemeny, "Emotions and the Immune System," *Bill Moyers, Healing and the Mind*, pp. 195-211.

10. Thomas Delbanco, "The Healing Roles of Doctor and Patient," *Bill Moyers, Healing and the Mind*, pp. 7-23.

11. Norman Cousins, "Tapping Human Potential," *Second Opinion*, July 1990, p. 56ff.

12. http://www.psychologytoday.com/articles/200504/laughter-the-best-medicine

13. Norman Cousins, *Anatomy of an illness as perceived by the patient: reflections on healing and regeneration*, (New York: Norton, 1979).

14. http://www.mda.org/Publications/Quest/q34laughter.html

15. Kevin Fedarko and Mark Thompson, "All for One," *Time*, June 19,1995, pp. 21-23.

16. Max Lucado, *The Eye of the Storm* (Dallas: Word Publishing, 1991), pp. 200-201.

17. Original story by Rick Weinberg of ESPN, http://sports.espn.go.com/espn/espn25/story?page=moments/94